READING DERRIDA READING JOYCE

The Florida James Joyce Series

Reading Derrida
Reading Joyce

Alan Roughley

University Press of Florida

Gainesville
Tallahassee
Tampa
Boca Raton
Pensacola
Orlando
Miami
Jacksonville

04 03 02 01 00 99 6 5 4 3 2 1

Library of Congress Cataloging-in-Publication Data

Roughley, Alan.
Reading Derrida reading Joyce / Alan Roughley.
p. cm.—(The Florida James Joyce series)
Includes bibliographical references and index.
ISBN 0-8130-1684-3 (alk. paper)
1. Joyce, James, 1882-1941—Criticism and interpreta-
tion—History. 2. Literature, Modern—20th century—
History and criticism—Theory, etc. 3. Derrida,
Jacques—Contributions in criticism. 4. Joyce, James,
1882-1941—Influence. I. Title. II. Series.
PR6019.09Z7865 1999
823'.912—dc21 99-19693

The University Press of Florida is the scholarly
publishing agency for the State University System of
Florida, comprising Florida A & M University,
Florida Atlantic University, Florida International
University, Florida State University, University of
Central Florida, University of Florida, University of
North Florida, University of South Florida, and
University of West Florida.

University Press of Florida
15 Northwest 15th Street
Gainesville, FL 32611–2079
http://www.upf.com

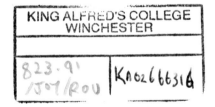

To the memory of
Professor Bernard Benstock
and
Professor Augustine Martin

CONTENTS

FOREWORD

Alan Roughley gives us the first full-length study of the relationship between Jacques Derrida's criticism and the works of James Joyce. The ten
chapters of his study fall into four sections. The first begins with Derrida's
dissertation on the dualism of empirical language in Husserl and proceeds
to the concept of marginality as it is used in Derrida's and Joyce's works.
Here Roughley considers linguistically unexpressed phenomena as they
stand unvocalized, and then their manifestations in language and as a part
of a history that is in itself transient and arbitrary. The result is a sort of
Husserl/Derrida antihistoricism that Derrida asserts was part of Joyce's
concern, particularly in *Finnegans Wake*, although Stephen expresses the
concept in the Nestor episode of *Ulysses*. In effect both Joyce and Husserl
attempt to recapture the ideal Platonic form. In the second chapter
Roughley interweaves Joyce's work with Derrida's concepts of Levinas,
Arnold, and Heidegger, all in the ultimate framework of Hegel's dialectical
opposites.

The three chapters of the second section discuss Joyce's less marginalized
relationship to Derrida's *Glas, Dissemination,* and *The Post Card: From
Socrates to Freud and Beyond*. One of the highlights of the section deals
with the lack of closure and the cyclical nature of the *Wake*. The chapters
of the third section, "Speaking of Joyce," investigate Derrida's spoken
words on Joyce within the context of the relationship between spoken and
written (or printed) language that is so important in both Derrida's work
and *Finnegans Wake*. They analyze what Derrida has said about Joyce on
three different occasions. The first fully reveals the profound influence of

Joyce on Derrida's work, while the second, on *Ulysses,* is framed in a circular pattern reminiscent of the *Wake,* with its insistence on the self-reflexivity of its own creative process. The third talk on Joyce explores the comedic *jouissance* that enables Joyce to enjoy, even as he satirizes, what serious Joycean scholars attempt to deconstruct. Roughley maps out Derrida's adoption of Joyce's playfulness and destabilization of his (Joyce's/Derrida's own) text. In his discussion Roughley further addresses the problem of Derrida's description of feminist appropriation of Joyce's language. The identification of Molly's beginning and ending of her monologue with the affirmative *yes* is both phallocentric and antiphallocentric, at the same time seeing Joyce's language and text as enclosed in a metalanguage "identified with the metaphoric female cycle of water" and ALP—the whole a confirmation of the female principle.

In the three chapters of his final section, Roughley, himself a deconstructive writer, offers a glossary of Derrida's terminology, such as "arche-writing," "the blank/hymen," "the book as ideological structure," "*différance,*" "double marks and the double bind," "grafting," "the gramme," "logocentrism, phonocentrism, and phallocentrism," and "the trigger." Roughley provides several practical applications of each term to the gamut of Joyce's fiction. Each application gives a wholly new informative interpretation to a section of Joyce's work and underscores the eminent worth of the entire topic of Derrida and Joyce in the clearest demonstration possible.

Zack Bowen
Series Editor

PREFACE

You is feeling like you was lost in the bush,
boy? You says: It is a puling sample jungle
of woods. You most shouts out: Bethicket me
for a stump of a beech if I have the poultriest
notions what the farest he all means.
FW 112.3–6

I dream of a writing that would be neither
philosophy nor literature, nor even contaminated by one or the other, while still keeping—
I have no desire to abandon this—the memory
of literature and philosophy.
Derrida 1992b:73

It may seem strange at this point in the history of Joyce studies to return to
an exploration of Joyce's writings from the spaces opened up by Jacques
Derrida in order to explore what goes on between the writings of Joyce and
Derrida. Joyce scholarship has moved on and "progressed" (or so the story
goes) to exploring Joyce from the perspectives of cultural studies. Deconstruction is passé. Even its very name seems no longer to serve any purpose,
having been superseded by such terms as *deconstructionism* or *deconstruc-*
tionalism. As critics like Jonathan Loesberg demonstrate, however, much
work remains to be done in understanding the full impact of Derrida's use
of an aesthetic, literary language in his philosophical investigations.
Derrida's reading of Joyce is of particular relevance to what Loesberg calls
"aestheticism as inherently an interpretation of historical and ideological
issues" (Loesberg 1991:9).

There is a problem with trying to categorize Derrida's work according to
the either/or distinction between literature and philosophy, at least until
Derrida's use of an aesthetic language in his philosophical investigations is
better understood. A further problem results from pigeonholing his work
with the philosophically foundational principles of teleology and linear
progression or the taxonomic systems of literature, philosophy, or critical
theory. Locating Derrida's work at some point along the linear chronology
of developments in the history of critical thinking—say somewhere between

structuralism and semiotics and neohistoricism—is analogous to placing Joyce's writing somewhere between Conrad and Golding in developments of the novel during the twentieth century.

Of course, Derrida and Joyce can be, and are, classified in this way, but only by setting aside the power of their respective achievements and the ways in which their writings subvert the very concepts and principles (presence, facticity, genre, teleology, progression, linearity) upon which such categorizing and classification are grounded. The writings of Joyce and Derrida rupture the taxonomic structures that are founded upon these concepts and principles. These ruptures are analogous with the gap into the unconscious opened by Freud, and the practice of criticism after Joyce and Derrida in some respects engages in the same project as the psychoanalysts who followed Freud. Lacan argues that the Freudian unconscious was forgotten as Freud foresaw it would be. It "closed itself up against [Freud's] message thanks to those active practitioners of orthopaedics that the analysts . . . became, busying themselves, by psychologizing analytic theory, in stitching up this gap" (Lacan 1978:23). Joyce criticism may have "moved on" and "progressed" beyond deconstruction, but it has done so by closing off or ignoring the conceptual ruptures and textual spaces opened up in the writings of both Joyce and Derrida. It is these ruptures and spaces, as well as the intertextual play between them, that are the subjects of this study.

Echoing Derrida's words, Rodolphe Gasché argues that Derrida's writings belong to both literary criticism and philosophy at the same time that they belong to neither. This study attempts to show how Derrida countersigns Joyce's writing as one that inhabits the same aesthetic textual topoi as his own. Derrida consciously situates his writings *between* philosophy and literature in order to explore what goes on between texts given those labels. At the same time, he interrogates the "archic" concepts (presence, mimesis, teleology, representation, and so on) upon which both literature and philosophy are grounded. While there is a clearly recognizable deconstructive method of literary criticism that can be located somewhere between structuralism and cultural studies in recent trends in literary studies, that method has surprisingly little to do with Derrida's writings.

The attempt to systematize Derrida's writings in order to produce a methodology for analyzing literary texts necessarily has to overlook (amongst other things) Derrida's questioning of the very process of systematization on which the deconstructive "method" of literary criticism is grounded. Questioning the founding concepts and processes of his own discipline is an important part of Derrida's writing, and such a preparatory examination of the boundaries of the critical discipline is noticeably lacking in much so-called deconstructive literary criticism. Discussing the relevance of Derrida's philosophy for literary criticism, Gasché states: "So-called deconstructive criticism, which . . . is but an offspring of New Criticism, has not, to my knowledge, undertaken these preparatory steps" (Gasché 1986:255).

Derrida's frequent bracketing of certain terms by placing them within the "double marks" traditionally reserved for speech, or "so-called" spoken text within writing, is part of his interrogation of key terms and concepts from his discipline of philosophy. His use of parentheses and his strategy of placing key terms such as *being sous-rature* or *under erasure* are also important techniques in Derrida's investigation of the horizons of philosophy and writing. The term *being* is for Derrida continually and continuously involved with the founding philosophical question of "What is?" Whether in an investigation of the individual existence of particular phenomena (the letters of a word, the construction of a book, the function of the pen inscribing writing) or as part of an investigation of Being as a philosophical concept, Derrida follows Heidegger in re-marking the term with crossed lines in order to remind us that the investigation of Being is the foundation of philosophy and one that is ongoing. Indeed, the notion of Being as an ongoing process of becoming would seem to be one of the reasons why Derrida finds Joyce's writings such a powerful attraction.

For Derrida, Joyce's writings are not only a part of what traditional literary criticism defines as literature, but also a series of powerful operations in what Derrida signifies as "Literature." Literature (outside the double marks) frequently relies on philosophical concepts—such as being and mimesis or representation (a concept philosophically defined by Plato, as we shall see)—that it rarely questions, but behaves as if it could confidently answer the question of what, exactly, these concepts signify; "Literature" suspends these concepts, identifies the necessity of investigating them, and then proceeds to do so.

Traditional literary characters are often presented to readers with an unquestioned and unquestioning reliance on the philosophical concept of existence or being (and indeed upon the process of representation by which language makes character "present" to the reader); the concept of being at work in "Literature" is continually investigated and called into question to remind us that the questioning of being is a primary, pressing, ongoing, and unfinished matter for philosophy and "Literature" alike. Joyce's writings investigate and interrogate the concepts of being upon which the presentation of characters in language is premised in numerous ways (for example, destabilizing identity, interchanging "novelistic" characters and those of the alphabet, creating a "being with a difference" [FW 269.15]), and Derrida's work is continually haunted by the ways in which they do so.

Insofar as it views itself as having "moved on" or "progressed" from deconstruction, contemporary cultural and historical criticism seems to confuse Derrida's writings with programs of systematic literary deconstruction. Derrida's writings work against such programs. Unfortunately, critics who have recognized this have sometimes mistakenly linked Derrida's work—and particularly his use of poetic or figurative language in philosophical investigations—with nihilism or antihistoricism.

Such an association might stem from Derrida's use of literary language in his exploration of the limits of philosophical logic and reason. Loesberg examines Derrida's use of aesthetic and literary language and finds no foundation for the criticism of Derrida as a nihilist: "Derrida's philosophical analysis . . . does not undo all constraints of logic and reason in favor of a nihilist free play, but rather identifies a necessary contradiction within philosophy's ambition to offer foundational rules governing all knowledge" (Loesberg 1991:7).

As we shall see in the course of this study, Derrida strongly denies the claim that his work is not historical. He firmly insists that he "is very much a historian, very historicist," and he rejects critics who accuse him of ahistoricism and believe that deconstruction is not concerned with history. Derrida is suspicious of those professional "historians" who are "naively concerned" with objectifying the "content of a science," and his work reveals serious reservations about any historicism that fails to consider the vital tool of language with which historicism gathers its evidence and then represents this evidence and the arguments premised upon it (Derrida 1992b:54, 55).

Cultural theory concerns itself with the production of literary texts as historical and cultural products. It is grounded on concepts of history and the historical developments of culture that are often refined and qualified but rarely, if ever, fully interrogated. Discussing Raymond Williams's definitions of culture, for example, John Storey concludes that the "principal function" of texts as cultural practices is "to signify, to produce or to be the occasion for the production of meaning" (Storey 1993:2). The concepts upon which meaning depends (presence, sense, reason, comprehension) are not an issue.

Like the systematic deconstructive criticism that Gasché identifies as a branch of New Criticism, cultural theory concerns itself with the systematic investigation of this cultural "production of meaning" rather than any investigation of what that "meaning" might in and of itself mean. The interrogation of the fundamental concepts on which meaning relies is an ongoing concern in Derrida's work and one that Derrida shares with the writer who transformed the title *The Meaning of Meaning* into "the maymeaminning of maimoomeining!" (*FW* 267.3).

Joyce's defamiliarizing of these words is also a decapitalizing of the title of the book by C. K. Ogden and I. A. Richards that investigates how so-called literary meaning is rhetorically and poetically produced and comprehended by the reader. Joyce's decapitalizing and defamiliarizing pun on the title robs it of its legal status as a title in a double process that invites the reader to interrogate how "the meaning of meaning" can lose its "original" meaning and gain an apparently new set of meanings while still maintaining its signifying play with the originary phrase. It also invites us to interrogate the process of mimesis at work in these (at least) double operations by the positioning of the phrase next to the botanical pun "Mimosa multi-mimetica" (*FW* 267.2–3).

Mimesis and the production of an always-at-least-double meaning sustained by the tension between the signified object and the very process of signification itself: these are the operations between Derrida's writings and his readings and re-marking of Joyce's texts that form the focus of this study. The function of thematic criticism is the elaboration of meaning according to the logic of the theme; the space between the concept of meaning and what meaning of that concept might be is a part of those double (and doubling) textual spaces articulated by Joyce and rearticulated, re-marked, and explored in Derrida's deconstruction.

What follows marks out those spaces between the lines of the texts from which the citations at the beginning of this preface have been taken in order to regraft them and set them to work in the hope of re-marking a small amount of the vast intertextual play going on between the writing practices from which they were removed and back to whose sites they continue to radiate. It is written for readers and lovers of writing who may have an interest in the writings of either James Joyce or Jacques Derrida, or both, and it should be of particular interest to anyone who has attempted to understand the impact that Joyce has had on Derrida's theories, or, to use Derrida's words, the ways in which "Joyce's ghost is always coming on board" Derrida's writing, "even in the most academic pieces of work" (Derrida 1984a:149). In focusing primarily on those parts of Derrida's writings and talks where Derrida is clearly offering a reading of Joyce, I have tried to tease out some of the ways in which Joyce's ghost comes "on board" Derrida's work.

This metaphor of the ghost is one to which Derrida returns in his work *Specters of Marx,* where he discusses the inability of traditional forms of scholarship to deal with the metaphorical concept of the ghost: "There has never been a scholar who really, and as scholar, deals with ghosts. A traditional scholar does not believe in ghosts—nor in all that could be called the virtual space of spectrality." The problems of dealing with ghosts are important in this study, and they manifest themselves in numerous ways. The problem caused for traditional forms of scholarship is a result of the ambiguous relationship that the notions of ghosts and haunting have with the philosophical concept of being: "There has never been a scholar who . . . does not believe in the sharp distinction between the real and the unreal, the actual and the inactual, the living and the non-living, being and non-being" (Derrida 1994:11). The medium for dealing with Joyce's haunting of Derrida's work would seem therefore to lie elsewhere than in the traditional forms of scholarship.

I was tempted to give this study the title *(Im)possibilities.* Readers who have struggled with Derrida's writings on Hegel's view of the relationships between a traditional preface and the other parts of a book in *Dissemination* might well have some understanding of this temptation. Borrowing Derrida's own technique of using his "double marks" to rewrite *confusion* as "(con)fusion," I had hoped that "(im)possibilities" might convey some sense of the double bind facing anyone writing on Joyce and Derrida. This double bind is produced by the impossibility of ever fully comprehending all of the polysemous meanings and complex textual operations of either of the two writers. Completing a book that might offer a fullness of meaning on two such powerful writers is an impossibility even if one dreams of the possibility of doing so.

Since Joyce, and perhaps even more since Derrida, our understanding of the form of a book as an ideological structure has been radically changed, and any attempt to discuss the relationship between these two writers within the traditional form of the book is in a certain sense doomed to failure. Both Derrida and Joyce have produced books without conventional structures or endings. They both teach us that our concept of the book as an ideological form as well as our ideas about the relationships between speech and writing can, and should be, radically rethought. Joyce's works are so frequently discussed with such literary terms as *short story, novel, epic,* and *plot and character* that it is easy to forget how radically Joyce has affected our understanding of those terms. Readers of *Finnegans Wake* are aware that its characters can be letters of the alphabet as well as imitations of living people, and it is in the spaces between literal inscription and mimesis that Joyce's writings challenge many of our conventional understandings about literature and writing. Joyce's narratives can be analyzed with the conventional Aristotelian concept of a plot as a unified structure with a beginning, middle, and end, but those same narratives also can be seen operating according to another logical structure, and this double structure explains one of the powerful attractions of Joyce's writings for Derrida.

Anyone who has attempted to write on Joyce will know the sense of failure with which that task can begin. While this might also be the case for writing about numerous other writers, with Joyce this sense of failure can be intensified by the feeling that anything one might try to say about Joyce's writing has already been said by that writing itself. This is a general predicament of all commentary and criticism, but the immense complexities of Joyce's writings make the predicament more obvious than it might be in the case of commentary on other writers. Derrida sums up the impossibility of writing on Joyce when he discusses the ways in which we are all caught in Joyce's "archive as in a spider's web" (Derrida 1984a:146). Stephen Dedalus may have thought he was capable of flying by the nets that Ireland threw up to prevent his soul taking flight, but anyone who tries to read *Finnegans Wake* will know that Joyce has flung up a series of nets from which there is no escape.

Finnegans Wake is a book that we can never finish reading in the same way that we can finish reading a book by other authors. This is because of the text's endless circularity. As Stephen Heath argues, there "is no conclusion to be reached in a reading of Joyce's text" (Heath 1984:61). The difficulties of analyzing and understanding Joyce's writing can be understood by a metaphor from the *Wake:* We punch another set of holes in the text with our critical forks, but then forget that we made those holes ourselves as we spend our time wondering about their significance in Joyce's text. Derrida summarizes the impossibility of finishing a reading of the *Wake* when he discusses how after even "twenty-five or thirty years" of trying to read Joyce's text, the reader must still "stay on the edge of reading Joyce . . . and the endless plunge throws you back onto the river-bank, on the brink of another possible immersion, *ad infinitum*" (Derrida 1984a:148).

A book on Derrida's reading of Joyce is also an impossible book to finish because the desire to create an endless encyclopedic form at work in Joyce's writing repeats itself in Derrida's work. It is possible to dream of completing a book on Joyce and Derrida, but even one simultaneous reading of *Finnegans Wake* and *Glas* is enough to turn that dream into a nightmare. It is not possible to finish reading the *Wake,* and deconstruction requires an "interminable analysis" that cannot be achieved by a "unilinear text, or a punctual *position,* an operation signed by a single author" (Derrida 1987b:42). All one can do is accept Derrida's necessity of reading and rereading "those in whose wake [he] write[s]." Rereading the authors whom Derrida reads and rereads also throws us back into Joyce's "jungle of woods," where we again find ourselves feeling as if we are "lost in the bush." One way of trying to find a path out of this bush is by occupying some of the marginal positions inscribed by Joyce and re-marked by Derrida in order to uncover some of the intertextual relays and circuits between the projects of these two writers. We will see how the powerful force of the marginal in Joyce—an importance already noted by several writers on Joyce—is adopted and modified by Derrida and set to work in his project of deconstruction.

Until *Dissemination,* Joyce seems to have occupied a marginal position in Derrida's writing, and, as we will see in examining that text, some critics still see Joyce occupying a marginal (in the sense of unimportant) position in his work. From Derrida's perspective, however, describing Joyce's position as marginal is not at all the same as saying that Joyce's work is unimportant. For Derrida, the term *margin* functions both as a signifier of the traditional border of the text and as a metaphor for the positions from which deconstructive readings and analyses can take place. As a result of deconstruction's overturning of the hierarchical terms of traditional binary oppositions (male and female; light and dark; good and evil; inside and outside; nature and culture) the operations of marginal inscriptions can rival and overshadow the importance of the central column(s) in terms of power, meaning, or importance.

Derrida's notions of marginality are at work in the ideas about the subversive margins of fictional texts defined by Shari Benstock: "footnotes in fictional texts do not necessarily follow the rules that govern annotation in critical texts: they may or may not provide citation, explication, elaboration, or definition for an aspect of the text; they may or may not follow 'standard form'; they may or may not be subordinate to the text to which they are affixed" (Benstock 1983:203–4).

Benstock was one of the first critics to link Derrida's notions of marginality with the operations of the marginalia and footnotes of *Finnegans Wake*'s tenth section. In her study of that section, Benstock discusses "Derrida's general concern for all that exists at the margins of discourse—literally and physically on the printed page as well as intellectually, linguistically, and psychologically in the act of writing." Benstock also notes that Derrida's concern with the margins of discourse is "frequently the stated subject of his writings" and is "also apparent in his own use of textual adjuncts" (Benstock 1983:220 n. 1).

Derrida's use of marginal positions as both a theme and a site for deconstruction offers new interpretative strategies as well as insights into the deconstructive operations within specific texts. In *Dissemination,* for example, Derrida's marginal concerns are manifest in the layout of some of the main text and footnotes. In his investigation of how traditional theories of mimesis can be subverted and transformed within the general play of textual dissemination, Derrida offers the ironic statement that it "is not possible for us to examine here the extremely complex system of Plato's concept of *mimēsis.*" He then proceeds to examine precisely how Plato's concept of mimesis is developed in the *Dialogues* and "forms a kind of logical machine" that "deals out all the clichés of criticism to come" (Derrida 1981: 186–87 n. 14). This mapping is done marginally in the five or so paragraphs of a footnote that requires the "main" text to occupy much less space on the printed page than does the footnote.

In "Implications," Derrida uses *margin* as a metaphor for the positions he occupies in the texts he deconstructs: "it is necessary to read and reread those in whose wake I write, the 'books' in whose *margins* and between whose lines I mark out and read a text simultaneously almost identical and entirely other" (Derrida 1987b:4; emphasis added). Whether or not the "wake" in this passage can be included with the several marginal allusions to Joyce's text that Derrida makes elsewhere, it will be helpful to keep the paradoxical importance of margins in mind as we look at Joyce's appearance in marginal positions within Derrida's work.

For both Joyce and Derrida, marginal parts of a text are capable of a force that produces important effects within the text's main body. The operations of this force can disrupt and overturn the traditional, hierarchical evaluation of the main body of a text as more important and powerful than its marginal counterpart. Derrida clearly identifies the marginal position as important for his own work in the passage cited above. In *Ulysses* both the jar of Plumtree's Potted Meat and the slogan advertising it are relatively unimportant in terms of the traditional emphasis placed on the novel's central characters and plots. Joyce's writing, however, gives this marginal textual fragment a power belying its status as a minor, realistic textual detail in the narrative by making the potted meat and its advertising slogan signifiers of humor, love, betrayal, and death, as well as the textual slippage that undermines a strictly representational reading of Joyce's text. He does this through repeating the ad in different contexts, and, as Astradur Eysteinsson demonstrates, the frequent repetitions "manipulate and change [its] significance," increasing the ad's power to disrupt and subvert the realistic narrative (Eysteinsson 1990:227).

In other words, the disseminative repetition of the minor or marginal elements of narrative that traditional criticism treat as realistic detail can have very powerful textual effects and disrupt even the philosophical and literary principles upon which such criticism is founded. The Plumtree slogan, for example, which could be treated as a relatively minor touch of realistic detail, triggers off a powerful interrogation of the very concept of mimesis or representation on which many careful readings of *Ulysses* have been constructed.

Although I used both Derrida's French texts and the English translations of his work in researching this study, I have written it in English for readers who are not averse to reading Derrida in translation. My purpose in writing the book has not been the production of an advanced linguistic study of the effects of translating either Joyce or Derrida, but an investigation of what goes on between their writings and a marking of some of the ways in which Derrida's readings of Joyce have affected the various writing strategies he has employed during the development of his various deconstructive theories. References to Derrida's texts are to the published English translations.

There is a sense in which Derrida seems to have had English readers in mind as an important part of the audience to whom he writes. The people for whom I wrote this study are not the linguists and other scholars with a valid academic interest in the nuances lost and gained in translation, but those readers, thinkers, students, and teachers for whom reading Derrida and/or Joyce remains an exciting, if continually daunting, challenge. Thinking of this audience, I am reminded of Blake's plea to the reader's of his *Jerusalem:* "Therefore [Dear] Reader, [forgive] what you do not approve" (Blake 1982:145).

Acknowledgments

This book would not have been possible without the work, the kindness, and the generosity of many Joyceans. Elliott Gose at the University of British Columbia supervised my dissertation on Derrida and *Finnegans Wake,* and I remain indebted to him for his interest and wise counsel. In addition to the work of Shari Benstock and Murray McArthur, both of whom have graciously permitted me to quote extensively from their writings, Margot

Norris's *The Decentered Universe of* Finnegans Wake: *A Structuralist Analysis* (1974) has been an indispensable study for everyone interested in Derrida's work as a context for reading Joyce. Christine van Boheemen's "Deconstruction After Joyce" (1988) followed in the footsteps of Benstock's work and emphasized Derrida's indebtedness to Joyce. The editors and writers of *Post-Structuralist Joyce* (1984) brought the importance of French readings of Joyce to everybody's attention, and Jean-Michel Rabaté, one of the contributors to that collection of essays, was extremely generous and helpful in his criticism of some of my earlier work.

There have been too many Joyceans to name who have helped me in my attempts at understanding Joyce, but conversations with Bonnie Kime Scott, Suzette Henke, and Sheldon Brivic have been particularly helpful. I thank John Bishop and Augustine Martin for some delightful and illuminating conversations in Dublin. Gus Martin and Terence Dolan gave me the opportunity to teach at some of the James Joyce summer schools in Dublin, where I discussed my ideas with the staff and students. Fritz Senn and Geert Lernout have been two of the best Blakean corporeal enemies for whom a reader of Joyce could have wished. Bernard Benstock encouraged me when, in his words, I felt "caught in the crossfire between theoretical and antitheoretical camps" of Joyce studies. Zack Bowen has been very generous and supportive in his comments on my work.

At University of New England in New South Wales, Julian Croft has been a good friend and a staunch supporter of Joyce studies in Australia. Brian Birchall, the most Hegelian of Australian philosophers, has proved an invaluable dialectical sounding board. My thanks to Sally Nicol for typing earlier drafts of the manuscript.

I completed the final drafts of this study while I was a visiting research fellow at the University of York. I am again indebted to the kind generosity of Jacques Berthoud, who made it possible for me to accept this honorary post at York so that I could complete the study. Liz Fleming deserves my thanks for the encouragement she gave to me at the University of East London. Megan Roughley deserves a special thank you for her generous help in the substantive editing, critical analysis, and corrective readings that were an essential part of the process by which this study was realized.

For you may be as practical as is
predicable but you must have the
proper sort of accident to meet
that kind of being with a difference.

FW 269.13–15

CHAPTER 1

Joyce in Derrida's Reading of Husserl

DERRIDA'S FIRST WRITTEN ENCOUNTER with Joyce took place around the same time he completed his first major work on the phenomenology of Edmund Husserl. Husserl's work was among Derrida's first philosophical interests, and Derrida found Joyce's literary writings valuable for providing an alternative perspective on Husserl's goal of phenomenological univocity. Derrida uses Joyce as a model and source in the development of the aestheticism with which "he outlines" the "problems . . . within the foundational movements of Continental Philosophy" (Loesberg 1991:7). These problems include those Derrida finds in Husserl's attempt to create an internal and univocal language by which the transcendental consciousness can "escape from language's externality" (Loesberg 1991:87).

In 1953–54 Derrida visited the Husserl Archives at Louvain and then completed his higher studies dissertation, "The Problem of Genesis in the Philosophy of Husserl." In 1956 he was awarded a grant as a "special auditor" to attend Harvard University on what Bennington describes as the "somewhat fictitious pretext of consulting microfilms of unpublished work by Husserl" (Bennington and Derrida 1993:329). Derrida spent much of this time at Harvard reading Joyce.

At the same time that he began work on *Edmund Husserl's* Origin of Geometry: *An Introduction,* Derrida began to draw on Joyce as an alternative model for the complex relationships among culture, language, and history he was investigating in Husserl. This date for the emergence of a significant interest in Joyce on Derrida's part is confirmed by the reference to Joyce in the study of Husserl and by Derrida's statement, in 1982, that "you stay on the edge of reading Joyce—for me this has been going on for twenty-five or thirty years" (Derrida 1984a:148).

Derrida positions Joyce next to Husserl in *Edmund Husserl's* Origin of Geometry: *An Introduction* because of their respective attitudes toward language and the ideal forms of history that were the focus of much of Husserl's work. The contrast with Joyce and his project of collapsing history into the synchronic, equivocal forms of writing appears in Derrida's explorations of Husserl's theories of language and their continual appeals to the imperative of univocity, or the unity of a single voice and signifier, in its relationship to objectivity.

In Husserl's project of developing phenomenology as a pure, nonempirical discipline, history is valuable to the extent that it facilitates the transmission and revelation of ideal, objective philosophical and mathematical forms from one generation of philosophers to the next. These forms are accessible as objects of consciousness (the basic and irrefutable existents) because of their objective and independent existence as correlatives of states of mind common to the thoughts of different minds in different cultures throughout different periods. For Husserl there "must be some objectivity in the origin of an ideality for the ideality to be recognisable" (Leavey 1989:13). This insistence on objectivity raises the question of how such an objectivity might be achieved. For Husserl the answer is linguistic. He seeks a univocal linguistic mode to provide the objectivity and make the ideality recognizable. He wants a form of language that will enable sense to obtain "its ideal objectivity" (Leavey 1989:13).

Derrida identifies three distinct linguistic levels of ideal objectivity in Husserl's work. The first is the *"primary"* level of the "word's ideal Objectivity." On this level, a specific word can be "free and therefore ideal," compared with its sensible, phonetic, or graphic incarnations only within a "facto-historical language." The word can be seen as "free" in that it is not dependent on, or identical with, any of its particular materializations. In whatever way it is manifested, the word is "always the *same* word which is meant and recognized" (Derrida 1989:67). At the same time, it remains interrelated with "the de facto existence of a given language." The word *royalty,* for example, might occur as an ideal form independent of its materialization in this queen or that duke or in any image of either. It is also "free" in that it is "recognizable" in different languages (*royauté*); but it still remains tied to the specific language in which it makes sense.

On a *"secondary"* and "higher degree of ideal Objectivity," a word's sense can be available in different languages through differing signifiers. This means that the ideality, the form of the idea (of something, for example, like a tree that can be signified by such differing words as "tree," *"arbre,"* or *"baum"*), is free "from all factual *linguistic* subjectivity" (Derrida 1989:70–71). In other words, the ideal concept or content of "tree" is independent of the subject (and subjectivity) of the utterance or expression (the speaker's identity, nationality, language, place and time, and so on). However, this ideality is "limited" in that, in spite of the content's independence from the subject, it remains tied to the natural, contingent reality of the tree encountered as a sensible object; that is, it "adheres to an empirical subjectivity" and is "empirically conditioned" (Derrida 1989:71).

The third level of "absolute ideal Objectivity" is the level of the free, ideal geometrical forms that are the ultimate object of Husserl's investigations. On this *"tertiary"* level, the "ideal Objectivity of geometry is absolute and without any kind of limit." The ideality of geometry is "no longer only that of the expression or intentional content; it is that of the *object itself*" (Derrida 1989:72).

Exploring this third level of ideality, Derrida uncovers what he sees as an essential paradox in Husserl's project: if the ideal objects-in-themselves do not require any specific languages to be expressed, how can they be revealed? He describes the paradox in the following way: "without the apparent fall back into language and thereby into history, a fall which would alienate the ideal purity of sense, sense would remain an empirical formation imprisoned as fact in a psychological subjectivity—*in the inventor's head.*" Furthermore, if the linguistic "historical incarnation sets free the transcendental, instead of binding it," then this "last notion, the transcendental, must then be rethought" (Derrida 1989:77). Pointing to the necessity of language for the expression of the ideal, and emphasizing the historical facticity of the ideal expressed in language, Derrida works toward deconstructing the fundamental Husserlian belief that ideal forms could be rediscovered through a practice of production if their accreted significations were somehow erased, rendering them no longer subject to written or spoken linguistic traditions, or history.

Husserl sees humankind living "in one and the same world" and potentially cognizant of the same ideal forms. That there are ideal forms, albeit signified by a variety of different signifiers from different languages, "establishes the possibility of a universal language" (Derrida 1989:79). This universal language of ideal forms both establishes and requires the univocity of singular ideal forms. It is within this context of the nature of the ideal and the functions of language in revealing ideal forms that Derrida compares the respective projects of Husserl, which insist on univocity, and of Joyce, which insist on equivocity.

Husserl's desire to eliminate equivocity is linked to what Loesberg describes as phenomenology's claim of a "decisive break with philosophy" and philosophy's complex, equivocal relationships with its own history (Loesberg 1991:86). Husserl's primary concern was "defining a transcendental consciousness." To eliminate the effects of philosophical and linguistic equivocity, he "first expels [equivocal and external] communication from the language of the transcendental consciousness" (Loesberg 1991:87).

For Husserl, Derrida contends, "equivocity always evidences a certain depth of development and concealment of a past" (Derrida 1989:102). To counter the equivocity of historical and philosophical language, Husserl "proposes an inward speech that enacts a pure, imaginative representation." This "pure representation" (were it possible) would transcend the equivocal (and paradoxically) concealing revelations of the past and transcend "any presumption of an outside object" and the limitations of external communication (Loesberg 1991:87).

Equivocity conceals the past because its "depth of development," its accretion of significations, obscures the historical idealities of the past even in the very process of (equivocal) signification by which it reveals them. The memory of a culture is equivocal in simultaneously concealing past events in the very process by which it attempts to reveal them. Furthermore, any individual attempt to remember or internally memorize the history of the culture is defeated in the attempt to gain full access to the ideal forms of that culture by the equivocity operating in the very language making the history of a culture accessible.

Given these conditions, Derrida suggests one has a "choice of two endeavours" one can make "when one wishes to assume and *interiorize* the memory of a culture in a kind of *recollection*" (Derrida 1989:102). One endeavor is the effort to locate the most univocal expression of a culture's memory and then strive for an equally univocal language in which to express the interiorized memory of that culture. The other is to account for, and attempt to take on board, the equivocity making a univocal access and expression of the culture's memory impossible. These are the two endeavors chosen respectively by Joyce and Husserl. Joyce attempts "to repeat and take responsibility for equivocation itself"; Husserl tries "to reduce or impoverish empirical language" to the point where its univocity is transparent (Derrida 1989:102, 103). Joyce strives for an overdetermined equivocity; Husserl, for a pure univocity.

The projects of Husserl and Joyce proceed from comparable antihistoricist positions. Derrida uses Stephen's famous comment about history from *Ulysses* as the basis for his creation of the "transcendental parallels" between the two, although it seems to be in *Finnegans Wake* that he sees Joyce's project attaining a status equal to that of Husserl. Drawing on Stephen's proclamation of history as "a nightmare from which [he] is trying to awake," Derrida applies Stephen's words to the projects of both writers, stating that "Husserl's project, as the transcendental 'parallel' to Joyce's, knows the same relativity" as Joyce's project.

Like that of Joyce, Husserl's project "proceeded from a certain antihistoricism and a will 'to awake' from the 'nightmare' of 'history' as well as a will to master that nightmare in a total and present resumption" (Derrida 1989:103). In Husserl, this antihistoricism entails the attempt to return to original ideal forms and overcome the limitations of their articulation in specific, historically determined forms; in Joyce, it is the attempt to bring the past into the present of a writing that seeks to collapse the chronological distance between specific historical events, myths, and narratives and to articulate these events synchronically in a metadiscourse describing itself as a "collupsus" of the "one thousand and one stories" (*FW* 5.27, 28–29) it tells, a "collideorscape" (143.28) in which historically specific myths and events collide in the continuous and contiguous presents of Joyce's narratives.

Husserl wished to uncover the ideal geometrical forms that are the original historical forms of all subsequent geometry; in Derrida's reading, Joyce wished to uncover the ideal forms of "mythology, religion, sciences, arts, literature, politics, philosophy, and so forth" (Derrida 1989:102). Joyce's project moves in the direction of the Hegelian ideal, encyclopedic and universal containing form; Husserl's in the direction of the pure, univocal ideal and original geometric form. Husserl's project moves toward revealing particular ideal forms; Joyce's toward revealing generalized ideal forms. Joyce strives for the medium of a universal language of equivocation that might be able to take on board the forms of all languages; Husserl, for the medium of a univocal language capable of rendering itself transparent so that it might somehow reveal the origins of geometrical forms without the mediation of language.

The paradoxical juxtaposition of Joyce and Husserl provides philosophical and literary support for Derrida's critique of neohistoricism. The purpose of Derrida's comparison of their projects is a delineation of their shared teleology, the respective, ideal, yet impossible languages for which they strive, and the different positions of relativity that both Husserl and Joyce had to adopt. Joyce's project entails repeating and taking responsibility "for all equivocation itself, utilizing a language that could equalize the greatest possible synchrony with the greatest potential for buried, accumulated, and interwoven intentions within each linguistic atom, each vocable, each word, each simple proposition, in all worldly cultures and their most ingenious forms" (Derrida 1989:102).

In contrast to this, Husserl's project is to rid language of all equivocation, to "reduce or impoverish empirical language methodically to the point where its univocal and translatable elements are actually transparent." The ultimate goal is to "reach back and grasp again at its pure source a historicity or traditionality that no de facto historical totality will yield of itself" (Derrida 1989:103). Husserl attempts to reach back and uncover this historicity; Joyce, to re-create it, to bring it into the present and wake it from the nightmare of history in which it slumbers.

Neither a pure univocity nor pure equivocity is possible, and therein lies another (asymmetrical) parallel between the projects of Husserl and Joyce. Husserl strove for a pure (and ultimately impossible) univocity but had to admit an "irreducible, enriching, and always renascent equivocity." Cultures are constructed by language and sustained and supported by a continual linguistic exchange in which intention and memory as well as meaning are realized through equivocity. Without equivocity the ideal would become "paralyzed" (such paralysis is detailed in *Dubliners*). Equivocity can thus be seen as the "congenital mark of every culture" (Derrida 1989: 103). In investigating the transmission of the ideal forms of geometry, Husserl was necessarily dealing with culturally transmitted forms of language even if he was seeking ways of access to the pure, original ideals of the geometrical forms.

Joyce's project of situating himself within equivocity, within as many diverse linguistic fragments from as many languages as possible, could "only succeed by allotting its share to univocity" (Derrida 1989:103). Incorporating all of the possible linguistic forms (written, spoken, phonetic, ideogrammatic, pictogrammatic, hieroglyphic, mathematical) from all languages into a single textual site is an impossibility. And even if it were possible to do so, the text repeating these forms "would have been unintelligible; at least it would have remained so forever and for everyone" (Derrida 1989:103).

What makes the numerous languages, puns, typographical unorthodoxies, geometrical figures, and sigla of *Finnegans Wake* intelligible to some extent is the incorporation of various univocal strands (the base language of English, the recognizable geometric patterns, the encoding of the sigla in English, the recognizable song rhythms, and so on) within the text. Husserl's desire for pure, original geometric forms is a desire for ideality; so, too, is Joyce's goal of creating a universal language for the "one thousand and one stories, all told, of the same" (*FW* 5.28–29). This shared desire for ideality and the antithetical direction of the projects in which it manifests itself is an important force in Derrida's paradoxical juxtaposition of the two writers.

Derrida's deconstruction of Husserl's *The Origins of Geometry* sets Joyce's writings to work as a corrective to the limitations of Husserl's aspirations for a pure ideal univocity, a univocity that is in the last resort unattainable. Nevertheless, it is Husserl's univocity and relativity that Derrida uses to define the teleology of both projects. Their respective projects are relative because the equivocity Husserl attempts to avoid is that for which Joyce strives and the univocity Joyce's project seeks to evade is that at which Husserl's project aims. But this relativity is not symmetrically balanced. Derrida contends that "[i]f the univocity investigated by Husserl and the equivocation generalized by Joyce are in fact *relative,* they are, therefore, not so *symmetrically.* For their common *telos,* the positive value of univocity, is *immediately* revealed only within the relativity that Husserl defined" (Derrida 1989:104). The equivocal project Joyce undertakes is not possible without the univocity desired by Husserl, for univocity is "that without which the very equivocations of empirical culture and history would not be possible" (Derrida 1989:104–5). It was the very univocity Joyce sought to avoid by situating himself in the midst of an overdetermined equivocity that made that equivocity possible.

Comparing the limited number of citations of Joyce with the vast amount of attention Derrida devotes to Husserl in *An Introduction* reveals Joyce's position as that of a marginal figure in relationship to a central figure. At the same time, Derrida's later notions on marginal positions as the positions from which deconstruction can get under way enable us to see that in his first major study Derrida is already assuming a marginal position in which he employs Joyce's writing to analyze and critique Husserl's project. The citation of one now well-known sentence by Stephen Dedalus and Derrida's summary of Joyce's project in the *Wake* (a summary revealing Derrida's interest in, and familiarity with, Joyce's final work) creates a marginal position in *An Introduction*. This paradoxically important marginal position situates Derrida in the margins of Joyce's text and sets his reading of Joyce to work in the center of his reading of Husserl. Overturning the traditional, hierarchical privileging of the center (of the subject, of his reading of Husserl, of Husserl's concept of history and the ideal), Derrida sets his reading of Joyce to work as he initiates one of the powerful rhetorical and textual strategies that mark his later writings.

CHAPTER 2

The Marginal Joyce in *Writing and Difference*

WE HAVE SEEN THE METAPHOR OF BEING haunted by Joyce's ghost that Derrida offers in "Two Words for Joyce": "every time I write, and even in the most academic pieces of work, Joyce's ghost is always coming on board" (Derrida 1984a:149). Using Joyce's ghost as a part of his project of pushing and expanding the borders defined by traditional concepts of being and existence (in both their literary and philosophical appearances), Derrida's metaphor of Joyce-as-ghost allows him to treat Joyce's name as he elsewhere treats the variously named forms of "to be" related to the philosophical concept of Being: placing them "under erasure" (Spivak 1976:xiv).

The questioning of the relationship between the name and the object it signifies, of the signifier and its signified, is a forceful strategy in Derrida's solicitation of the concept of being and philosophical definitions of existence and the structures of existence. In *Specters of Marx* Derrida further develops the notions of ghost and haunting as a part of his project of soliciting and interrogating the concept of being. The logic governing a ghost's haunting enables Derrida to bring the idea of otherness or alterity to his investigation. Discussing haunting in terms of the "first time" and repetition, he argues that haunting is marked as "[a]ltogether other. . . . This logic of haunting would not be merely larger and more powerful than an ontology or a thinking of Being. . . . It would harbor within itself . . . eschatology and teleology themselves" (Derrida 1994:10).

Derrida's technique of placing certain terms under erasure mimics the strategy suggested by Heidegger, in *The Question of Being*, of drawing crossed lines over the word *Being*. For Heidegger, drawing these crossed lines over the word "wards off . . . especially the habit of conceiving 'Being' as something standing by itself." It is also linked to exposing the "presumptuous demand that [thinking] know the solution of the riddles and bring salvation" (Spivak 1976:xv). Placing the signifiers of being, like the verb *to be* or *is*, under erasure allows the negative other of the signifier to come into play. As Derrida says of the assertion "reading *is* writing": "this oneness designates neither undifferentiated (con)fusion nor identity at perfect rest; the *is* that couples reading with writing must rip apart" (Derrida 1981:63–64).

The metaphor of Joyce's ghost haunting Derrida's deconstructive investigations of the concept of being brings into play the force of Joyce's writing upon Derrida's investigations at the same time that it suggests something of the significance of Joyce in Derrida's work. In *Writing and Difference* Joyce's ghost haunts Derrida's writing from marginal positions, and, as a ghost, Joyce both is and is not an important force.

In the essays of *Writing and Difference,* as in Derrida's reading of Husserl, Joyce's positions are marginal. The first of these is in the footnotes to the essay "Force and Signification," where Derrida investigates the distinction criticism makes between itself and its object in terms of force: "Criticism henceforth knows itself separated from force, occasionally avenging itself on force by gravely and profoundly proving that separation is the condition of the work, and not only of the discourse on the work" (Derrida 1978:5). In the footnote to this passage he offers a meditation on the traditional distinction between the "creative force" and "the critical act."

This meditation recites Flaubert's proposition that "'One writes criticism when one cannot create art'," and, following that proposition, the list of unproductive relationships between writers and critics. The recitation ends with "And when the translation of Hegel is finished, Lord knows where we will end up." Derrida claims that "Flaubert was right to fear Hegel" and cites Heidegger's quotation of Hegel's criticism of art: "'its form has ceased to be the highest need of the spirit'." Following the recitation of Flaubert and Heidegger's citation of Hegel, Joyce's name appears as a signifier of a creative force in a most marginal position, situated between Proust and Faulkner, as one of the writers who can be explained by the fact that the translation of Hegel (out of German certainly, but also out of Hegelian terms into those that might make Hegel easier to comprehend) "hasn't been finished" (Derrida 1979:302 n. 4).

This marginal citation of Joyce is important in juxtaposing the writer with Hegel as Derrida earlier juxtaposed him with Husserl. It also somewhat ambiguously offers the notion that Joyce might, or might not, have read Hegel—"The difference between Mallarmé and these other writers is *perhaps* the reading of Hegel" (Derrida 1978:302 n. 4; emphasis added)—and that Joyce might be "explain[ed]" by the unfinished business of Hegel. The metaphor of haunting explains this possibility of Joyce as "perhaps" a Hegelian writer, for the possibility exists on the very border belonging to haunting: "between the real and the unreal, the actual and the inactual . . . in the opposition between what is present and what is not" (Derrida 1994:11).

The possibility of some kind of link between Hegel and Joyce interests a number of Joyceans, but empirical historians in the Joycean community are frustrated by the difficulties of trying to take a precise *measurement* of the extent to which Derrida sees Joyce as a Hegelian ghost. Geert Lernout, a critic who strongly disagrees with the idea of Joyce as either a Hegelian writer or a major power in Derrida's writing, notes that the "linking of Joyce and Hegel had originally been suggested by Jean Paris" in 1957 and "has been elaborated since by a great number of critics," including Jacques Aubert, Jean-Michel Rabaté, Alain David, and Geoffrey Hartman (Lernout 1990:59).

We will consider the significance of Derrida's linking of Hegel and Joyce later in this chapter and elsewhere in the book. The point here is the reliability of the empirical historicism that dismisses Derrida as "reliable witness on Joyce" (Lernout 1990:61). This is not a claim Derrida makes for himself, but one Lernout claims Derrida is making. Elaborating the French critical context for Derrida's linking of Joyce and Hegel, Lernout cites Joyce in his attempt to dismiss Derrida's reading of Joyce as grounded on "faulty reasoning, 'woman's reason' or oxymoron." Trying to recontextualize Derrida's deconstructive reading into the limited terms of a historical empiricism founded on utilitarianism, Lernout argues that Derrida's reading is "questionable" because Derrida is citing the words of Lynch and those words "cannot in any *useful* sense be taken as the expression of the author's opinions" (Lernout 1990:34; emphasis added). This invocation of a univocal, linguistic transparency (words are the transparent medium for the expression of their user's ideas) applies the Husserlian historicism Derrida finds deconstructed in Joyce's writing in order to place Joyce back into the very nightmare of historicist empiricism from which Stephen Dedalus wished to awake and out of which Joyce successfully wrote himself.

The second essay haunted by Joyce's ghost is, appropriately, an investigation into madness exploring the limitations of Descartes's cogito in defining madness as a state of being. "Cogito and the History of Madness" deconstructs Michel Foucault's "Madness and Civilization: A History of Insanity in the Age of Reason." It demonstrates how Derrida's ex-teacher's view of madness was limited by its reliance on the Cartesian idea of the cogito in its attempt to define madness. While consciously situating himself in the position of an ex-disciple, Derrida states that he retains "the consciousness of an admiring and grateful disciple" (Derrida 1978:31). For this exploration of madness, Derrida marginalizes a comment Joyce made about the writing of *Ulysses.* In the left-hand column at the beginning of the essay, Derrida inscribes Kierkegaard's statement "The Instant of Decision is Madness." Just below this, and directly in line with the title, *Folie et déraison: Histoire de la folie à l'âge classique,* Derrida positions, "In any event this book was terribly daring. A transparent sheet separates it from madness. (Joyce, speaking of *Ulysses*)" (Derrida 1978:31).

With these two citations, Derrida creates a textual play that Joyce himself had already employed and foregrounded in *Finnegans Wake:* a marginal, polysemous use of words and phrases simultaneously signifying in several different directions. One of the conclusions at which Derrida arrives in this essay is that all critical decisions entail a crisis in which there is an exposure to at least the possibility of madness: "But the crisis is also decision, the caesura of which Foucault speaks, in the sense of *krinein,* the choice and division between the two ways separated by Parmenides in his poem, the way of logos and the non-way, the labyrinth, the *palintrope* in which logos is lost; the way of meaning and the way of nonmeaning; of Being and of non-Being" (Derrida 1978:62). This moment of decision, which opens the possibility of madness, can be linked to the apparition of the ghost whose appearance takes place on "the very borders between being and non-being, between what is and what is not." This is something Derrida explores in identifying Hamlet's questioning "to be or not to be?" as a fundamentally philosophical question that is linked to the apparition of the ghost in Shakespeare's play (Derrida 1994:10–11).

The reading of Descartes that Derrida offers as a supplement to Foucault's distinguishes two aspects of the Cartesian cogito that can and must be separated in the "crisis of decision." The first is the spectral aspect, the "non-way," the "labyrinth" and palintropic, hyperbolic project of the Cartesian cogito. Possessing a "mad audacity," this hyperbolic project entails the "return to an original point which no longer belongs to either a *determined* reason or a *determined* unreason, no longer belongs to them as opposition or alternative" (Derrida 1978:56). The second aspect is that "which belongs to a factual historical structure" (Derrida 1978:60).

Derrida's interest in the projects of Husserl and Joyce can be considered in the context of these two aspects of the cogito, for both writers—Husserl through univocity and Joyce through equivocity—sought to escape the limited determination of the "factual historical structure[s]" of their respective traditions in order to return to the "common origin" of the "zero point," where "all determined contradictions, in the form of given, factual historical structures, can appear, and appear as relative to this zero point at which determined meaning and nonmeaning come together in their common origin" (Derrida 1978:56).

The crisis of decision in which the choice between these two options is made is the crisis of Hamlet, who experiences *krinein,* or the Kierkegaardian mad instant of decision, in his encounter with the irrational, with the simultaneous being and nonbeing of his father's ghost, an encounter rearticulated in *Ulysses* and employed as a framing device in Derrida's *Specters of Marx*. Citing Joyce's words on the transparent sheet separating *Ulysses* from madness brings Joyce's ghost on board Derrida's reading of his teacher's thoughts on madness, but the teacher was unable to approach madness because unlike Joyce's "transparent sheet," the Cartesian ego is an opaque block keeping madness from Foucault's sight even as it allows him to think of it as a possibility: "*I* who think, I cannot be mad" (Foucault, cited in Derrida 1978:55).

The possibility of reading through the transparent sheet separating *Ulysses* from madness keeps the possibility of seeing this madness in play. The words of Joyce's ghost, of Joyce's name as a signifier of "Being and non-Being" articulate a madness that can be kept at bay yet still seen. These words of Kierkegaard and Joyce situated in the margin at the beginning of Derrida's essay anticipate such conclusions even as they simultaneously engage in a play with each other *and* with the words in the main, right-hand column of the essay that constitute the introduction. They offer a way of meaning when read as signifiers of each other and of nonmeaning (for each other) when read as separate and distinct signifiers of the main column of Derrida's text.

The ways in which these citations are involved in an intertextual play with each other, with the opening words and with the concluding words of the essay, are not unlike the ways in which the marginalia operate in the *Wake*'s lessons section. At the beginning of 2.2, for example, the left-hand marginal inscription *"with his broad and hairy face, to Ireland a disgrace"* (FW 260.lh), signifies the "big-guard" who is "shot" (FW 260.6–7) in the central column of the text as well as the variations on the adult male figures who appear in the left-hand column after the initial figure with the *"hairy face."*

At the same time, this figure is also involved in a signifying play with the list of patriarchs, philosophers, and biblical figures who appear in the left-hand margin on the section's penultimate page (307), as well as with the "Pep" figure addressed in the "NIGHTLETTER," with which the section concludes. All of these figures are treated as the targets of antiphallocentric forces and restage the movement of Hamlet against Old Hamlet and Claudius; of Stephen Dedalus against the fatherly priest and king he must kill in his mind; and of Shem, Shaun, and Issy against HCE. In *Specters of Marx* Derrida uses the appearance of the ghost from Hamlet to elaborate his theory of "hauntology" (Derrida 1994:10); in "Cogito and the History of Madness" he raises the specter of his old, paternal teacher in order to exorcise it from his own investigation of madness.

The general theme of overcoming the father (by taking his place, going beyond him, or symbolically killing him) found in *Hamlet* and rearticulated in Joyce's *Ulysses* and Derrida's writing is important throughout the *Wake*. The same theme is restaged by Derrida in his overcoming of the teacher who had once held a pedagogic and parental position in Derrida's time as a student. The opening words of "Cogito and the History of Madness" refer to Foucault's study of madness as a "point of departure" for the "reflections" on madness and reason that constitute the essay. This "point of departure" involves the *critical* moment in which Derrida decides to leave the work of his ex-teacher to reexamine it critically from a point that would not have been possible when he was still in the position of a student.

Kierkegaard's pronouncement on the instant of decision as an opening of the possibility of madness signifies the moment when the conscious decision to part from the teacher is made. The decision "not . . . to dispute, but to engage in dialogue with the master" produces a state of melancholia—"an unhappy consciousness" (Derrida 1978:31). This unhappiness is "interminable" and comes from the student having to think of what has been present as an absence: it "stems from the fact that he does not yet know—or is still concealing from himself—that the master, like real life, may always be absent" (Derrida 1978:32).

Derrida doubles the madness of Kierkegaard's decision with the possible Joycean madness that is separated from *Ulysses* by a "transparent sheet," and, as the essay reveals, the "transparent sheet" operates as a metaphor for the position between the Cartesian cogito and the madness that it tries to comprehend. As the creator of *Ulysses*—and this seems to be one of the reasons for Derrida's use of the Joycean fragment—Joyce is aware of his text as "other"—as the use of a language that would have been madness had it not become *Ulysses*. In becoming the cogito that is "assured of what it says," the Joycean cogito takes the "terribly daring" critical decision to risk madness in becoming the "other" that is the language of *Ulysses* in its totality. What Derrida says of language in general holds also for the particular language of Joyce: "being the break with madness, it adheres more thoroughly to its essence and vocation . . . if it pits itself against madness . . . and gets closer . . . to it: to the point of being separated from it only by the 'transparent sheet' of which Joyce speaks, that is, by itself" (Derrida 1978:55).

Derrida positions Joyce's words in a precise alignment with the title of Foucault's book, a title occupying the position of the "other" to both the comments by Kierkegaard and Joyce, as well to Derrida's views on Foucault's inability to comprehend madness because it is always in the position of the other to the Cartesian cogito. The words "In any event this book was terribly daring. A transparent sheet separates it from mad—" are divided into three lines that are in an offset alignment with two lines in the central column constituted by the words "Foucault's book *Folie et déraison: Histoire de la folie à l'âge classique*." The effect of the offset alignment creates the possibility that Joyce's words can signify the title of Foucault's text, the "transparent sheet" referring to the marginal "paperspace" between Joyce's spectral words and the title of Foucault's text.

The Joycean "other," marginal textual fragment, separated from the central text by the blank space between them, signifies Foucault's failure to escape the limitations of the Cartesian cogito in his effort to comprehend madness. From Derrida's perspective, the madness Foucault fought to define ultimately remains in the position of the other because Foucault followed the Cartesian cogito along the path of the "factual historical structures" but failed to follow it along the "non-way" of the hyperbolic project. Governed by the necessarily linear, historical model of the Cartesian cogito,

Foucault's "History of Madness" remains an empiricist history of the madness that the neoclassical period sought to define and regulate under the control of the rational cogito. It failed to grasp the phenomenological essence of madness because it could not see that madness as its own alterity.

The position of the subject (of the individual, of the theme, of the idea) in relationship to the totally other is at work in "Violence and Metaphysics: An Essay on the Thought of Emmanuel Levinas." Derrida investigates the thought of Levinas as it moves from agreement with some of the ideas of Husserl toward an acceptance of other ideas (and ideas of the other) from Heidegger, a movement Derrida interprets as a forceful movement away from Husserl as other. Both Husserl and Heidegger occupy the position of the other, even as Levinas uses two central Heideggerean themes against Husserl. The first is "the idea . . . that in the ontological order the world of science is posterior to the concrete and vague world of perception, and depends upon it." This theme is used to attack Husserl's vision "in this concrete world [of] a world of perceived objects above all" (Derrida 1978: 87).

The second attack against Husserl: "if Husserl was right in his opposition to historicism and naturalistic history, he neglected 'the historical situation of man . . . understood in another sense'." This "other" sense (and the sense of the other *qua* other) lies in the factual historicity Levinas finds Husserl neglecting. The correction to such neglect is found in the "'historical situation of man . . . understood in another sense';" that is, in the "historicity and temporality" which is "'the very substantiality of his substance' . . . '[T]his structure . . . occupies such an important place in Heidegger's thought'" (Derrida 1978:87).

The structure of the essay is that of alterity, of the relationship between the subject and its other, and this structure provides the context in which Derrida explores the development of Levinas's thought as it moves from an agreement with Husserl to an agreement with Heidegger (and then on to a disagreement with Heidegger's ontology). This structure is already at work in the passage from Matthew Arnold's *Culture and Anarchy,* which, like the citations from Kierkegaard and Joyce in "Cogito and the History of Madness," is inscribed in the left-hand margin at the beginning of the essay: "Hebraism and Hellenism—between these two points of influence moves our world. At one time it feels more powerfully the attraction of one of them, at another time of the *other;* and it ought to be, though it never is, evenly and happily balanced between them" (Derrida 1978:79; emphasis added). The Hebraic and Hellenic function as totally other for each other as well as for the world as each in turn becomes the other in whose "influence moves our world."

Derrida also uncovers the structure of the one and the other at work in two initial stages of Levinas's thought: the Husserlian and the Heideggerean. These reflect two major forces developing out of Hegel's thinking. These two forces articulate the differences between "philosophy as a power and adventure *of* the question itself and philosophy as a determined event or turning point *within* this adventure" (Derrida 1978:81).

Using the structure and play of Hegelian dialectic in which the antithesis operates as the other of the thesis until it is sublated and brought into the thesis and set to work until another antithesis arises, Derrida structures his essay to trace a variety of thetic-antithetical patterns. These include the dialectical development of Levinas's thought as it moves from a Husserlian thesis to an anti-Husserlian acceptance of parts of Heidegger's ontology and then on to an almost Husserlian rejection of Heidegger. They also include the larger, subsuming dialectic of the Hellenic/Hebraic pattern within which Derrida traces the development of Levinas's thinking and which Derrida suspends above the entire essay by inscribing it in the margin of the opening passage. And, at the end of the essay, following the repetition of an idea about Joyce that he offered in the notes of the first essay in the collection, that Joyce *might* be an Hegelian novelist—"*perhaps* the most Hegelian of modern novelists" (Derrida 1978:153; emphasis added)—Derrida offers the "neutral proposition," the peculiar synthesis, of Joyce's *Ulysses:* "'Jew-greek is greekjew'." For Derrida, this proposition articulates Joyce's project in *Ulysses* as one that moves between precisely the two poles of the Hellenic and Hebraic identified by Arnold in the marginal citation Derrida places at the beginning of "Violence and Metaphysics."

The conclusion toward which "Violence and Metaphysics" leads is that the thought of Levinas feels, in the words of Arnold, "more powerfully the attraction" of Hebraism than of Hellenism: Levinas "totally renews empiricism, and inverses it by revealing it to itself as metaphysics" (Derrida 1978:151). The empiricism of Levinas is an empiricism creating "an irruption of the totally-other; and nothing can so profoundly *solicit* the Greek logos—philosophy—than this irruption of the "totally-other"; and nothing can to such an extent reawaken the logos to its origin as to its mortality, its other." This irruption of the "totally-other" may also be the "experience of the infinitely other Judaism" (Derrida 1978:152).

Derrida's sense of Judaism's alterity as the other of the Classical Greek and the Christian traditions occurs periodically throughout his work, and we will look at it further in the context of *Glas* as well as in Derrida's speaking on Joyce. Derrida is attentive to Bloom's status as a Jew, a status that consigns Bloom to the role of the other in the Dublin of *Ulysses,* and Derrida's interest in Bloom's Judaism is never far from his concerns with that text.

In his counterpart to Bennington's text in *Jacques Derrida,* Derrida meditates upon his own Jewish identity and heritage as part of his mourning for his mother, consciously marking his place within the Classical and Christian traditions as the place of the other. At the same time, he appropriates the form of Augustine's *Confessions* for his own "circumfession," using the coincidental, biographical detail of his having dwelled literally in the place of the other by virtue of his family's residence on the "Rue Saint Augustin, Algiers" (Bennington and Derrida 1993:5). He also pursues his own Judaism in his discussion of the relationship between Joyce's writings and the academic reception of those writings, where he identifies himself with Bloom's identification as "ben Bloom Elijah" and points out that he "too [is] called Elijah: this name . . . was given me on my seventh day" (Derrida 1992a:284).

Derrida's interest in Levinas and the latter's attraction to Hebraism helps account for Derrida's attraction to Levinas's thought. Hebraism plays a major role in Levinas's "encounter with the absolutely other." This encounter is an essential part of Levinas's eschatology. It is "*the* encounter, the only way out, the only adventuring outside oneself toward the unforeseeably-other." Ethically, this encounter entails a "renunciation of hope." Indeed, within Levinas's *La trace de l'autre,* "eschatology does not only 'appear' hopeless," but "is given as such." Renunciation "belongs to its essential meaning" (Derrida 1978:95).

For Derrida, Levinas's encounter with the other cannot be experienced except as a trace because there "is no way to conceptualize the encounter." While it is "*present* at the heart of experience," it is only made possible "by the other, the unforeseeable 'resistant to all categories'" (Derrida 1978:95). The encounter is an ethical establishment of simultaneous relation with, and separation from, the other, and it is a "being-together as separation" that "precedes or exceeds society, collectivity, community." Levinas's term for it is *religion,* and this religion "opens ethics" because, for Levinas, the "ethical relation is a religious relation."

This religion is not one religion amongst others but a transcendent religion making it possible to accept separation (without hope) from the other as the only relation with the other. It is "*the* religion, the religiosity of the religious"; and it reveals the radical relationships between theory and ethics and the beginning of metaphysics that emerge when theory begins the critique of itself as ontology: "Metaphysics begins when theory criticizes itself as ontology, . . . and when metaphysics . . . lets itself be put into question by the other in the movement of ethics" (Derrida 1978:96). The renunciation of hope is an ethical movement toward the totally other, and the relation of separation from the totally other is the ethical relation which Being has with the totally other.

One trajectory followed by "Violence and Metaphysics" moves along the theme of Hebraism toward Joyce's version of the relation between being and the other within the context of the Hellenic/Hebraic antithesis. The meeting of Bloom and Dedalus is a staging of the same play between Hellenism and Hebraism at work in the Arnoldian citation Derrida cites at the beginning of his essay and expressed in the citation of Joyce that ends the essay: "'Jewgreek is greekjew. Extremes meet'." Hebraism and Hellenism and Jewgreek provide the frame for the entire work.

Derrida ends (but does not conclude) the essay with undecidability—the undecidability of the relation between Hegel and Joyce, "perhaps the most Hegelian of modern novelists," and the ultimate undecidability of the relations between the Jew and Greek: "does the strange dialogue between the Jew and the Greek, peace itself, have the form of the absolute, speculative logic of Hegel. . . . Or, on the contrary, does this peace have the form of infinite separation and of the unthinkable, unsayable transcendence of the other?" (Derrida 1978:153).

Setting to work the power of undecidability that increases in force during the course of his later work, Derrida finishes the essay with a final question on the meaning and legitimacy of the copula *is* in Joyce's proposition: "And what is the legitimacy, what is the meaning of the *copula* in this proposition from perhaps the most Hegelian of modern novelists: 'Jewgreek is greekjew. Extremes meet'?" (Derrida 1978:153). Derrida's "undecidables" are examined in the final chapter of this study, but one answer to the final question of Derrida's essay on Levinas that has already been cited is worth reciting as an end to this second chapter: the "oneness" signified by the copula *is* "designates neither undifferentiated (con)fusion nor identity at perfect rest; the *is* that couples [the subject and proposition of a sentence; reading and writing; "Jewgreek" and "greekjew"] must rip apart" (Derrida 1981:63–64).

CHAPTER 3

Movements from the Margins

Dissemination

THIS CHAPTER TRACES THE SPECTRAL
positions Joyce's ghost occupies in *Dissemination*. Like those we have already examined, these are again marginal positions; but the effects of Joyce's haunting of *Dissemination* are more readily discernible than the effects of that haunting in Derrida's earlier texts. Several interrelated, general themes link together Joyce's haunting of *Dissemination, The Post Card,* and *Glas:* the structure of the book as an *ideological* structure, the relationships between speech and writing, the relationships between fathers and sons, and the operations of desire in writing.

In all three texts Derrida is concerned with the question of the structure of the book as an ideological structure founded on the concept of the notion of unity (of the book and its component parts) and its tripartite pattern of beginning, middle, and end. This concern is apparent from the opening sentence of *Dissemination:* "This (therefore) will not have been a book" (Derrida 1981:3). One implication of this for our reading of *Dissemination* and the *Wake* is the establishment of a context for comparing the respective deconstructions of the ideological form of the structure of the book by Joyce and Derrida.

In *Dissemination* Derrida focuses specifically on the structure of the book as an ideological form determining the material ways in which the book is ordered and its language typographically displayed. Even a cursory glance at the way in which the column from Plato's "Philebus" is positioned next to a passage from Mallarmé's "Mimique" in the initial pages of *Dissemination*'s "The Double Session" reveals the possibility for an intertextual play between these passages similar to the one made possible by the "grouped textual field" of the *Wake*'s "lessons" section (2.2).

The ostensible source for Derrida's interrogation of the traditional structure of the book is the introduction to Hegel's *Phenomenology of Spirit*. In the opening section of this work, Hegel examines the traditional structure by which the introductory preface begins a book as an ideological pattern, and, according to Derrida, Hegel's conclusion is that "for a philosophical text as such, a preface is neither useful nor even possible" (Derrida 1981:11).

Hegel's dismissal of the preface is based on the premise that the sort of explanatory summary an author might offer in a preface "seems not only superfluous but, in view of the nature of the subject-matter, even inappropriate and misleading." This is because "whatever might appropriately be said about the philosophy in a preface — say a historical *statement* of the main drift and the point of view, the general content and results, a string of random assertions and assurances about truth — none of this can be accepted as the way in which to expound philosophical truth" (Hegel 1977:1). Derrida sees the relationship between the preface or introduction and the body of the book in terms of a struggle between, on the one hand, the labor of the concept constituted by the philosophical exposition that is the body, and, on the other, the exteriority of this labor that is simultaneously its summary and anticipation in the preface. The argument presented in the book *is* the philosophy; the summary in the preface is only *about* it.

This distinction can be related to the double bind of mimesis Derrida discusses in *Dissemination* and explores in his readings of Joyce. As we will see, mimesis, or representation, strives to say something *about* the object being represented in language under the guise of making that object present again (re-*present*ed) *in* language. In deconstructing the traditional, hierarchical privileging of thought over speech and speech over writing, Derrida investigates how representation is founded upon the philosophical concept of presence. He questions the sufficiency of that concept to account for the distinction between a linguistic articulation *about* a particular subject and one that claims to make that subject present. Chapter 8's examination of textual operations in *Ulysses* that Derrida's "undecidables" can signify explores how Joyce re-marks the operations of this double bind in his narrative.

Derrida argues that "[i]f the foreword is indispensable, it is because the prevailing culture still imposes both formalism and empiricism." This "culture must be fought, or rather 'formed' . . . better, cultivated more carefully. The necessity of prefaces belongs to the *Bildung*" (Derrida 1981:11–12). Derrida has described his own participation in attempting to fight or better "form" the prevalent cultural insistence on the preface and the traditional ideological concept of the book as one of the primary concerns of his own writing: "In what you call my books, what is first of all put in question is the unity of the book and the unity 'book' considered as a perfect totality, with all the implications of such a concept. And you know that these implications concern the entirety of our culture" (Derrida 1987b:3).

Derrida finds Hegel's contribution to the philosophical struggle with the idea of the unity of the book so important that he describes Hegel as "the last philosopher of the book and the first thinker of writing" (Derrida 1976:26). Hegel's work marks a transition between writing enclosed in the ideologically prescribed form of the book and a rethinking of writing that questions the forms in which it is presented. Joyce, whom we have seen Derrida describe as "perhaps the most Hegelian of modernist novelists," has also had a major impact on Derrida's rethinking and rewriting of the form of the book.

Derrida's deconstruction of the traditional form of book in *Dissemination* is clearly influenced by his reading of Joyce's *Wake;* but some Joyce scholars take a cynical view of the idea that the second section of *Dissemination,* "Plato's Pharmacy," is "nothing but a reading of *Finnegans Wake*" (Derrida 1981:88 n. 20). Such cynicism has done little to disprove Derrida's initial claim or his later reiteration of it: "I had the feeling that without too much difficulty one could have presented *La Pharmacie de Platon* as a sort of indirect reading of *Finnegans Wake,* which mimes, between Shem and Shaun, between the penman and the postman, down to the finest and most finely ironized detail, the whole scene of the pharmakos, the pharmakon, the various functions of Thoth, th'other, etc." (Derrida 1984a:150). As this chapter will attempt to show, Derrida's reading of the *Wake* is not concerned with proving he is a "Joycean expert" (Derrida views this phrase as something of an oxymoron) but with restaging, or "miming," some of that text's articulation of certain mythemes and the positions of some of their major characters.

In all fairness to empiricist critics, their primary concern is with historical, empirical textual matters. One of Geert Lernout's main objections to Derrida stems from what he terms "Derrida's characteristically unhistorical" readings (Lernout 1990:60). Derrida's claim, however, is that Joyce's "*ghost* is always coming on board . . . every time [he] write[s]" and "even in the most academic pieces of work," and it is easy to see the difficulties empiricists would face in trying to deal with the metaphor of Joyce's ghost (Derrida 1984a:149; emphasis added).

Derrida addresses such critics when he stresses the historical grounding of his own work: "Contrary to what some people believe or have an interest in making believe, I consider myself very much a historian, very historicist. . . . We must constantly recall this historical solidarity and the way in which it is put together" (Derrida 1992b:54). As we saw in his comparison of Joyce's equivocity with Husserl's univocity, Derrida is very concerned with the ways in which historical solidarity can obscure the very historical figures it strives to reveal. Joyce and Husserl offer antithetical modes for remembering and interiorizing culture and history within their writing, but Husserl's univocal ideal was as impossible to achieve as Joyce's perfect equivocity. Husserl could not rid the language he used of equivocity any more than Joyce could take on board all languages, myths, and narratives.

In comparing the projects of the two writers, Derrida's critique of the sort of historical and empirical proof demanded by critics such as Lernout is that the "pure historicity" sought by both Husserl and Joyce cannot be produced by the complicity of an empiricism and historicism that ignores the ways in which they themselves represent history: "no de facto historical totality will yield [historicity] of itself" (Derrida 1989:103).

Finnegans Wake performs a very Hegelianlike dismantling of the historically determined, traditional ideological structure of the book, and Derrida has described "Plato's Pharmacy"'s relationship to the *Wake* as "the most modest, the most miserable descendant of a corpus" (Derrida 1984a:150). As "modest" and "miserable" as this relation might (ironically) be, it would be surprising if Joyce's ghost were not haunting the structures of the text in which "Plato's Pharmacy" offers its deconstructive solicitation of the rules and compositions of texts, language, and writing.

In setting out to deconstruct the ideology that would enable *Dissemination,* or indeed any of his other "books," to be read according to the traditional rules of linearity and teleology that govern and determine the structures of the book, Derrida is doing little more than re-marking the achievements of both Hegel and Joyce in making their readers rethink how the ideological structure of the book restrictively determines and limits the play of the writing it contains and in reiterating the deconstructive and disruptive effects of those achievements within his work.

Finnegans Wake's formal solicitation of the traditional structure of the book is evident in its fusing together of its own "beginning" and "end." It is well known that the *Wake*'s final words constitute the first half of a sentence that ends on the text's first page. The complete sentence is "A way a lone a last a loved a long the" (*FW* 628.15–16) "riverrun, past Eve and Adam's, from swerve of shore to bend of bay, brings us by a commodius vicus of recirculation back to Howth Castle and Environs" (*FW* 3.1–3). Much has been made, in a literary context, of the circularity that this broken sentence achieves by allowing the reader to link the ultimate and initial words of the text, and it has been noted that the circular pattern achieved by this sentence has the effect of giving the *Wake* at least a double structure. The book has seventeen discrete sections that are frequently referred to as chapters. From another perspective determined by the logic of the ideology of the structure of a book, the *Wake* also has sixteen chapters or sections, one of which contains both the beginning and the end.

According to the rules regulating the concept of a book as a unity and totality, no part of a book can be greater than the book as a whole. The traditional form and logic of the book dictate that a book is greater than the chapters of which it is composed; that a chapter is greater than the sections and paragraphs constituting it; that a paragraph is greater than the sentences which constitute it; and that the sentence is greater than its constitutive words and letters. If this is the case, then because the *Wake*'s ultimate and initial words constitute one sentence, the final and first chapters of Joyce's text constitute one single chapter or section. This means that the number of sections is sixteen. The same is true for the number of "books" into which the *Wake* is divided. The traditional view that it consists of four books must be modified if the last section is a part of the first section because of the sentence fusing them together. Joyce, in fact, makes us think the impossible formulas $17 = 16$ and $4 = 3$, for his text has both sixteen *and* seventeen chapters as well as three *and* four sections. The text also makes us rethink the relationships of the "beginning" and "end" and of the "inside" and "outside" of the book, for if the sixteenth section and the third part contain both the "end" and the "beginning," they must metaphorically contain also that which is between the end and the beginning: the "outside" of the book.

For much of *Dissemination* (as well as in many other places within his work), Derrida focuses on the concept of the "double mark"—of double quotation marks, of the relationship between a model and its mimetic "double," and of that between the interior and exterior of the philosophical concept. In discussing Hegel's creation of a preface that "he *must* write, in order to denounce a preface," for example, Derrida argues that Hegel's preface "must be assigned two locations and two sorts of scope." In other words, the preface has "double" locations and scopes. Hegel's preface "belongs both to the inside and to the outside of the concept." However, "according to a process of mediation and dialectical reappropriation," which it was a part of Hegel's genius to articulate, "the inside of speculative philosophy sublates *its own* outside as a moment of negativity."

Derrida sees this articulation of the "prefatory moment" as part of an essential "lesson of Hegel's to be maintained, if possible, beyond Hegelianism": "The prefatory moment is necessarily opened up by the critical gap between the logical or scientific development of philosophy and its empiricist or formalist lag" (Derrida 1981:11). To maintain Hegel's lesson "beyond Hegelianism," Derrida moves from the model of dialectical sublation to the nonconcepts of (con)fusion and contamination. "(Con)fusion" signifies the ways in which grammatical subjects and predicates, and the inside and outside (of concepts, of texts, of writing) can be joined together without losing their individual identities in the consolidation of sublation. "(Con)fusion" is not the lack of order signified by "confusion" (although it is a pun on that term) but a "fusion" of one term with ("con") another (and its "other"), which allows both to retain their individuality and difference while being fused together, and to contaminate each other through their proximity, as a parasite contaminates the body of its host.

If Joyce's ghost is haunting and contaminating Derrida's own attempt to evade the repressive strictures of the ideology of the book in the writing of *Dissemination,* it is surely through Joyce's own monumental achievement of the *Wake* as a "double" writing practice in which the unity of the book is threatened and disturbed by its "Doublends" (*FW* 20.16), the two endings of the book undermining the single beginning and ending demanded by the traditional bibliographic model of unity. "(Con)fusion" offers a useful signifier of the *Wake*'s relationship with its own exteriority. The *Wake*'s first and last pages "(con)fuse" its initial and ultimate words into a single sentence. (Con)fusion is also appropriate for signifying the reading process that links the first and last pages of the *Wake* together through that sentence, requiring the reader to turn from the final page to the first in order to complete the sentence. This entails a metaphoric folding back of the book's cover so that the outer cover would successfully enclose the phallic column of its spine (a metaphor Derrida employs in *Glas*). An alternative model could be the articulation of the first and final words of the text as "A way a lone a last a loved a long the [THE OUTSIDE OF *FINNEGANS WAKE*] riverrun, past Eve and Adam's, from swerve of shore to bend of bay, brings us by a commodius vicus of recirculation back to Howth Castle and Environs" (*FW* 628.15–16;3.1–3).

The first model is sustained by ALP's last "leaf": "My leaves have drifted from me. All. But one clings still. I'll bear it on me. To remind me of. Lff!" (*FW* 628.6–7). This "one" leaf is of course at least two—a double (and Dublin) leaf, the mimetic imitation of a leaf from a tree on the banks of the Liffey *and* the linguistically self-reflective last leaf, or page, of the text on which the word is printed. The one floats on top of the river; the other bears the inscribed, or printed, marks of ALP's "leaves" upon itself. (In "Plato's Pharmacy," Derrida notes the doubling significance of the "'leaf': a significant metaphor, . . . or rather one taken from the signifier face of things, since the leaf with its recto and verso first appears as a surface and support for writing" [Derrida 1981:112].) This last page is also a prefatory page as it bears the last words that ALP-as-Liffey pronounces *before* she runs into Dublin Bay, and the last words of the text as it prepares the reader to return to the beginning of a new cycle of the book. It is very much like a page of Hegel's preface: "Yes—if—Hegel writes beyond what he wants to say, each page of the preface comes unglued from itself and is forthwith divided: *hybrid* or *bifacial*." In so far as a reader chooses to end a reading of the text with the final page, he will be able to re-mark a traditional linear narrative following Aristotle's prescription of the tripartite beginning, middle, and end pattern; if he chooses to link the first and last part of the sentence together, he will be able to experience how the text's circular narrative, with its "*bifacial*" ending/preface, confounds that ideological prescription, re-marking its own "other" form (and the form of its other) in its alterity.

"Plato's Pharmacy" is the section of *Dissemination* Derrida describes as a "reading of *Finnegans Wake*," and it is on this one sentence from a footnote of Derrida's essay that Lernout bases his criticism of Derrida as a reader of Joyce. The footnote offers the following observations: "The paragraph that is about to end here will have marked the fact that this pharmacy of Plato's also brings into play [*entraîne*] Bataille's text, inscribing within the story of the egg the sun of the accursèd part [*la part Maudite*]; the whole of that essay, as will quickly become apparent, being itself nothing but a reading of *Finnegans Wake*" (Derrida 1981:88 n. 20). Lernout picks up on the ambiguity of the phrase "the whole of that essay" and points out that the "prime referent" for the "essay may well be the essay of Bataille and not 'Plato's Pharmacy'" (Lernout 1990:60).

Lernout's argument is complex and refers to several different versions of Derrida's essay, but the thrust of his argument holds even for the 1968 and 1972 editions, where the footnote appears as number 17 rather than 20, and the phrase "that essay" is translated as "this essay." However, the playful ambiguity that Lernout treats as a historical and empirical problem is precisely that very force that the writings of Joyce and Derrida continually exploit as a most powerful linguistic and creative resource. In "Two Words for Joyce," for example, Derrida follows Joyce in exploiting the "double genitive" in the phrase "of *Finnegans Wake*" to describe his essay as one that simultaneously offers a "modest" reading *of* Joyce's text *and* "was read in advance" *by* that text: "This double genitive implied that this modest essay was read in advance by *Finnegans Wake,* in its wake or lineage, at the very moment that *La Pharmacie de Platon* was itself presenting itself as a reading-head or principle of decipherment (in short another software) for a possible understanding of *Finnegans Wake*" (Derrida 1984a:150). Derrida values Joyce's writing because of the play of such plurivocity as well as the strategies it offers for deconstructing unilinear and teleologically determined models of writing.

The third part of "Plato's Pharmacy" is "The Filial Inscription: Theuth, Hermes, Thoth, Nabû, Nebo," and Derrida recites as one of the three epigraphs for the section a passage from *A Portrait of the Artist as a Young Man:* "A sense of fear of the unknown moved in the heart of his weariness, a fear of symbols and portents, of the hawk-like man whose name he bore soaring out of his captivity on osier woven wing, of Thoth, the god of writers, writing with a reed upon a tablet and bearing on his narrow ibis head the cusped moon" (Derrida 1981:84). Derrida uses this passage as a prelude to his investigation of themes and figures that are also articulated by Joyce's writing, and particularly *Finnegans Wake:* the role of Thoth, the god of writing, who can use the ambiguity of the term *pharmakos* to outwit the patriarchal Ammon Ra by emphasizing its ambivalent semantic values of "poison" or "medicine" according to his own desires; the relationships of fathers and sons and of speech and writing, as well as of writing and memory, of the self and the other, and of the inside and the outside of texts. Derrida uses the passage from *Portrait* as a part of his strategy of mapping out "the internal, structural necessity which alone has made possible such communication and any eventual contagion of mythemes" (Derrida 1981:85). These mythemes are precisely those articulated by the writings of both Plato and Joyce.

In "Two Words for Joyce" Derrida returns to the same themes and figures, seeing in *Finnegans Wake* a rearticulation of the relationships between Thoth and the "others" of Thoth (troped in the *Wake* as "thother" [*FW* 224.33] and "th'other"[*FW* 452.13]), like Horus, Osiris, and Seth within the relationship between Shem and Shaun, "which mimes, down to the finest and most finely ironized detail, the whole scene of the pharmakos" (Derrida 1984a:150). Thoth is a marginal and powerful figure in *Finnegans Wake,* and as the god of writing, he is very significant to Joyce. Although Thoth is the brother of Osiris, he also participates in Seth's plan to kill Osiris in the well-known story of Osiris's dismemberment. Joyce condenses the story of Horus's revenge for his father's murder into "*How to Pull a Good Horus-coup even when Oldsire is Dead to the World*" (*FW* 105.28–29), one of the "many names" (*FW* 104.5), or alternative titles, for the *Wake* as they are troped as ALP's "untitled mamafesta" (*FW* 104.4).

"Plato's Pharmacy" also reveals Derrida's interest in contamination—in the ways in which the myths and narratives of different cultures contaminate each other, the ways in which literature and philosophy contaminate each other, and the ways in which writing may be seen as contaminating speech. In the second section of "Plato's Pharmacy," "The Father of Logos," Derrida explores the contamination of Greek philosophy by the Egyptian myth of the story of Thamus (the Greek god Ammon) and Theuth, or Thoth, as well as Ammon's fear that speech and memory will be contaminated by the "discipline" and "*pharmakon*" of writing Theuth presents to Thamus/Ammon. Thamus/Ammon is "god-the-king-that-speaks" (as opposed to one who might write), and Derrida sees his refusal of writing as a parental refusal: "The *pharmakon* [writing] is here presented to the father and is by him rejected" (Derrida 1981:76). The rejection of writing by the god-king-father who speaks has the effect of linking writing with the absence of the father and, eventually, with the patricide that enables writing to take place.

A part of Derrida's interest in the *Wake* stems from Joyce's completion of the project initiated by Thoth, and that project is mapped out in the various texts explored in "Plato's Pharmacy." Thoth's *pharmakon* of writing can replace the speech that the god-king-father wishes to protect; but for writing to take place, the father must be killed. In the *Wake,* HCE must and does fall. Shem the penman takes the place of his father and appropriates his father's pen/penis to write when he starts to "root with earwacker's pensile in the outer of his lauscher" (*FW* 173.9–10). This "outer" is both the outer part of Shem's ear and the "other" ear of the reader or listener ("lauscher") who must practice Stephen Heath's "optical listen" (Heath 1984a:58) in order to hear the speech that is overturned and set to work within the writing of Shem's "letter selfpenned to one's other" (*FW* 489.33–34).

The same figures and narratives of Egyptian myth that Joyce takes from *The Egyptian Book of the Dead* and refigures in *Finnegans Wake* are investigated by Derrida as he examines Plato's texts. Joyce refigures the god, Ammon Ra, in the pun "Enel-Rah": Shaun-the-Post's "head has been touched by the god Enel-Rah" (*FW* 237.27–8). Derrida is interested in Ammon Ra's origin as "the great falcon, hatched from his egg" as well as in the description of the "egg of the great cackler" (Derrida 1981:87). Joyce invokes the return of "the Great Cackler" who "comes again" (*FW* 237.34), weaving that figure into the narrative of the hen, Biddy Doran, who discovers both the *Wake* and the letter that figures within it (and the *Wake* is in turn figured by the letter) while pecking at the midden heap. Derrida examines the importance of the "egg of the great cackler" in the context of the "power of speech" as a power that is "one with the power of creation" (Derrida 1981:87), and Joyce has Biddy (herself a creator of eggs) discover a portion of the "Wake," which is a written text bringing its language to operate on the very borders between speech and writing: the written, inscribed, printed language brings within itself and sets to work paronomasia and the similarities in *sound* of spoken language.

For both Joyce and Derrida, writing is a "filial inscription." The father produces the spoken word, whose value is guaranteed by the presence of the father. As a "living thing, logos issues from a father" (Derrida 1981:143); writing is "the miserable son" (Derrida 1981:145). Both Joyce's Shem and Theuth of the Egyptian myths contaminating Plato's texts are the sons who must write. Thoth declares himself to be "the eldest son of Ra" (Derrida 1981:87). In the *Wake,* Shem, the son of ALP and HCE, writes down the letter uttered by ALP for HCE: "Letter, carried of Shaun, son of HeK, written of Shem, brother of Shaun, uttered for ALP, mother of Shem, for HeK, father of Shaun" (*FW* 420.17–19). Joyce uses the same double genitive that Derrida explores so that Shem is both the writer of the letter *and* its subject: the letter is one *of,* or by, Shem, and it simultaneously tells a tale of, or *about,* Shem and his family.

One of the fundamental features of the Earwicker family romance is that HCE has fallen into sleep and death and continues to fall throughout the narrative. As Macool and Finnegan, he is mourned at the wake and interred as the "brontoichthyan form outlined a-slumbered" (*FW* 7.20–21). It is ALP's desire that HCE "stand up tall! Straight." (*FW* 620.1), but ALP flows out into her own "cold mad feary father" (*FW* 628.2) before he does so, and the reader is thrown back to the first page in order to experience the fall of Finn again. Shem, the son and penman, writes the tale telling of the violence against his father ("it may half been a missfired brick" [*FW* 5.26]) that turns Joyce's book into a "cubehouse" rocking as "earwitness to the thunder of [HCE's] arafatas" (*FW* 5.14–15). Shem bears "earwitness" (5.14) to Earwicker in Joyce's "soundconducting" (*FW* 183.09) narratives, but HCE's voice sounds only as a muffled memory as Shem's failings are revealed: "the son—or patricidal writing—cannot fail to expose himself, too" (Derrida 1981:146).

Derrida sees "Plato's Pharmacy" as a "modest essay" that "was read in advance" by Joyce's text (Derrida 1984a:150). His articulation of "the whole scene of the pharmakos" is thus a re-marking of the site of the pharmakos as that site is already woven into Joyce's writing. In the warfare between Shem and Shaun as Glugg and Chuff, Glugg-Shem is also Thoth, the "thother brother" (*FW* 224.33). In the tale of the Ondt and the Gracehoper, the Ondt is figured as Thoth when he is "*thoth*fully making chilly spaces at hisphex affront of the icinglass" (*FW* 415.28; emphasis added). Shem the penman is identified with Thoth because Shaun-the-post is a "postal cleric," and Shem-Thoth, or "Thot's," "never the postal cleric" (*FW* 485.36). During the reverie that begins with an address to his sister, Issy, Shaun, in his role of Jaun, links Thoth with the "other" and the "author," as well as with Howth, where HCE's head is buried, and with the site of the family home in Chapelizod: "just thinking like *thauthor* how long I'd like myself to be continued at Hothelizod" (*FW* 452.9–10; emphasis added).

In this Jaun passage, Issy is "Sissibis" (*FW* 452.8), which links her with Thoth, who has the head of an ibis, as well as with the Egyptian goddess Isis. Elsewhere, however, ALP is linked with Isis through the operations of the double genitive that Derrida also employs. In replacing the Christian god with ALP, the *Wake* declares that "Anna was, Livia is, Plurabelle's to be" (*FW* 215.24). Plurabelle possesses being because of the genitive apostrophe, but as the apostrophe also signifies the missing "i" of "is," she also *is* being. ALP has being and, simultaneously, *is* being: She *is* to be, or "is" "is." This identification is again set to work in ALP's monologue when she declares, "What will be is. Is is" (*FW* 620.32). The pun on the name of Isis and the doubled "is" of the present-tense verb is also repeated after the declaration that "it is always tomorrow in toth's tother's place" and a pun on Ammon and "Amen" (*FW* 570.12–13): "Here we shall do a far walk (O pity) anygo khaibits till the number one of sairey's place. Is, is" (*FW* 570.28–30).

Although "Plato's Pharmacy" offers few explicit references to *Portrait* and *Finnegans Wake*, the mythematic, figural, and conceptual articulations of Derrida's writings offer "other" evidence of Joyce's haunting of *Dissemination* (and of his powerful force, along with Plato's and Hegel's, as the "other" of Derrida's text) as well as an intimation of the effect of that haunting on the works to come, "tomorrow in toth's tother's place." Assuming a filial position toward Joyce as his other, as the father of his own writing, Derrida situates himself in the margins of Joyce's text and reworks, re-marks, and reiterates some of the ways in which Joyce weaves the story of Thoth as father, brother, author, and other into his own version of the "one thousand and one stories, all told, of the same" (*FW* 5.28–9).

CHAPTER 4

Postcards to Joyce

THE DOUBLE STRUCTURE PRODUCED IN
the distance between the assertion of metaphysical premises and proposi-
tions and the ironic detachment from them is a "trait, or rather *retrait*" that
"would far exceed the periodizations of 'literary history' . . . from Homer to
Joyce, before Homer and after Joyce" (Derrida 1992b: 50). It is the effects of
such double structures (assertions and ironic detachment) or traits as they
operate between Socrates and Plato, Socrates and Freud, Freud and Joyce,
and Joyce and Derrida that are re-marked in the enigmatic and playful
messages inscribed on the back of Derrida's fictitious, philosophical, and
literary postcards.

The Post Card's solicitation of the ideology of the book is staged through
its identification of itself as a series of related postcards rather than as a
unified book; the *Wake*'s identification of itself as a letter, rather than a
book, written by Shem the penman and carried by Shaun the post, haunts
Derrida's meditations on postcards and postal systems as well as his ideas
on the relationships between writers, their writings, and addressees.

Derrida uses the figures of Socrates and Plato to explore the relationship
between Shem and Shaun as well as his own relationship with Joyce, a

relationship we shall see Derrida discuss in terms echoing the filial position in which he explores Plato's relationship to Socrates. *Dissemination* and *The Post Card* are obviously linked together by the figures of the two classical philosophers. In the "Plato's Pharmacy" section of *Dissemination,* Socrates is the teacher in the position of the father whose teachings determine and haunt Plato's texts but who comes to play a filial role himself in the texts written by his pupil. Within those texts, however, Socrates, as the son of his creator, in turn "supplements and replaces the impossible *noesis,* the forbidden intuition of the face of the father (good-sun-capital)" (Derrida 1981:167). In *The Post Card,* the relationship between Socrates and Plato is the subject of an extensive meditation that takes as its starting point the configuration of these two characters as they are represented on the front of the text in the illustration from the Bodleian Library's engraved frontispiece of Matthew Paris's thirteenth-century "fortune-telling book," *Prognostica Socratis basilei.*

In *The Post Card* the "author" of the postcards declares "never have I been so delirious" (Derrida 1987a:17). This delirium is a form of madness akin to that which Derrida explores in his deconstruction of Foucault's reliance on the Cartesian cogito and his exploration of the moment of decision and the possibility of madness that the instant of the *krinein* produces. Derrida's postcard readings engage in the "madness" of hyperbole that produces the "delirious" readings of the relationships between Plato and Socrates (in which Plato "is pushing himself off on a skateboard" or "taking tram fares in a poor country" [Derrida 1987a:17]). Plato and Socrates are figured as "S. and p." (Derrida 1987a:13), and, as Shari Benstock points out, S. and p. are also figured as "Shem the penman and Shaun the postman" (Benstock 1984:173). This figuring of Socrates and Plato as Shem and Shaun is already operating in *Dissemination,* As we have seen, Derrida describes "Plato's Pharmacy" as an "indirect reading" of the *Wake,* miming, "between Shem and Shaun, between the penman and the postman, down to the finest and most finely ironized detail, the whole scene of the pharmakos" (Derrida 1984a:150).

Shari Benstock and Murray McArthur have produced in-depth investigations of the relationships between Joyce's writing and Derrida's *The Post Card,* and their work is essential to an understanding of how Joyce haunts Derrida's work. While summarizing some of their important insights into Derrida's text, this chapter draws on the Joycean and Derridean technique of doubling in order to read some of Benstock's insights as a context for McArthur before moving on to consider some of the ways in which Derrida invokes the specters haunting his writing in order to establish their alterity as doubles of his own work. This rhetorical strategy entails assuming the position of Socrates to Joyce's Plato, thereby reversing the position assigned to him by McArthur.

In what is perhaps the closer reading of the two, Shari Benstock structures "The Letter of the Law: *La Carte Postale* in *Finnegans Wake*" by reproducing the double patterns from Joyce's text that Derrida has already employed. Within the two sections produced with this strategy, Benstock unfolds various structural and reading principles produced by the *Wake* and *The Post Card* respectively. Starting with an initial "frame-up," Benstock compares "The Ballad of Tim Finnegan" with Joyce's use of the song and shows how the "complexity of allusive levels in this title suggests the compacted linguistic structure of Joyce's text, a structure that cannot contain the multiplicity of its own meaning [and] whose borders are overrun by excesses of language" (Benstock 1984:163).

Following this "Frame-Up," and using a playful combination of Joycean and Derridean strategies (note, for example, how Benstock's title places *La Carte Postale* inside *Finnegans Wake*), Benstock offers the following "frames" that "have already shaped our reading of *Finnegans Wake*":

1. The missing apostrophe in the title. This "breaks" the frame of the "Ballad" for our reading and simultaneously produces a "pluralizing and playfulness of grammatical structure that opens up rather than encloses our reading of the text."

2. The circularity of the *Wake*'s narrative. Joyce's text appears to have a "sealed, internalized, whole, perfect and complete" structure, but this means that there is no beginning, no one opening into the text. As a result, the reader "always seems to stand both inside and outside its dimensions" (a double position echoing Derrida's assertion that "there is no outside to the text"), and "[t]here are too many answers to the question, 'where does it begin?'" (Benstock 1984:164).

3. Within the larger circular pattern of the *Wake*, the reader encounters intersecting points with smaller, circular narrative units: "There are stories within stories, each telling imbedded in another frame of receding concentric rings." In the "cyclic structure . . . one always reads 'through' the ring in search of the structure of the next ring." The traditional reason for this structure has been that the *Wake* is a dream. Benstock sees this raising as many questions (about the dream, the dreamer, "entrances and beginnings, of access to information, of lost origins and obscured sources") as it answers, so she

advocates a "multiple 'frame of reference' allowing for a maximum number of correspondences between dreams and letters" (Benstock 1984:165–66).

4. There are multiple readings of the *Wake*'s dream, and a "single reading translates instead into a variety of readings as the dream events shift, disperse, regroup and transfer themselves." Like so-called "real" dreams, the *Wake*'s dream cannot be fully recovered, and "the sources . . . are obscured." The identity of the dreamer, the particular events of the dream, its settings and particularities will always involve uncertainty because the "purposeful ambiguity of dream and reality—a persistent factor of the dream situation—turns the dream structure back on itself, shifting its borders" (Benstock 1984:166–67).

5. The ambiguities of the dream and reality are "carried over" to the frame of the letter with which the text metonymically identifies itself. This results from (and helps to cause) a "confusion of [the letter's] textual limits." The letter "contains all the versions of the dream story, comprises all the tellings of the tale, and includes all the letters of the *Wake*—those written by the children, the letter found by Biddy the hen in the midden heap, and various anonymous letters" (Benstock 1984:168).

6. The letters (missives and alphabetic letters) are also "nightletter[s]," "frames" with which the *Wake* attempts "to translate the dreamer and dream subject into the letter and its potential reader." It is here that Benstock begins to link Joyce and Derrida through the operations of desire as it is expressed in dreams, encoded in writing and then distributed through the postal network in *The Post Card*. What she says of the dream and the letter can be applied to the expression of desire in Derrida's postcards: "the story the letter tells rests on . . . a series of exchanges: the structural frames of the dream and the letter [and of Derrida's "desire" and his "postcards"] 'correspond to' the relationship between the unconscious and the conscious, between the states of sleeping and waking" (Benstock 1984:168–69).

7. Desire is the "missing 'content'" of the *Wake*'s letters, and this desire is "repressed so that it can only be acted out in dreams or acted on through writing." Desire follows circuitous paths in which it is displaced and transferred onto alternative "others." Benstock links the expression, transmission, and network of desire circulating throughout Joyce's text with the postal network traversing (and traversed by)

Derrida's postcards: "This trajectory of desire, which is also a system of *postes*, begins in the necessity to discover desire's destination and authority, to chart the space between desire and its object, to act out the sexual impulse for which dreaming and writing are only transferences. To trace the path of this desire, to follow the system of the *postes*, is to discover desire and its object, to know the destination of the love/lust letter, and to know why it must always be lost" (Benstock 1984:169–70).

These "frames" are mirrored by a series taken from Derrida's *The Post Card.* Like the series of letters in Joyce's texts, Derrida's postcards provide a "frame of reference for analysis of the components of correspondence, destination, desire and authority." Explaining that the reader is, in "lieu of a definition," "given reading options that seem to correspond to writing options that [she herself] took up and (perhaps) discarded," Benstock maps out the "multiple purposes" of Derrida's *envois*, or postcards. These include the possible relationships between a series of postcards and the preface for a book; the links forged by the writing, sending, and receiving of the postcards; the question of the authority of the postcard's sender and its (intended) receiver; the double roles that we play as readers of *The Post Card* and as readers of individual postcards (Benstock 1984:171).

Like the "frames" of the *Wake,* Derrida's frames, or "multi-purposes," serve to dismantle each other even as they sustain a relationship with each other. The "initial frame of reference, the postal card," for example, "is dislodged even before our reading of the postal cards has commenced" (Benstock 1984:172). The proliferation of the postcards undermines a systematic analysis of how the postcard in general might operate even as it makes the pretense of performing that analysis.

The postcard of the cover, for example, is a continual point of reference for many of the postcards constituting *The Post Card,* yet it is in a certain way a sham, or forgery, because it is a postcard that is an imitation of what it depicts. As the acknowledgment reveals, the cover illustration is "courtesy of the Bodleian Library, Oxford." It depicts "Plato and Socrates" from the "frontispiece of *Prognostica Socratis basilei,* a fortune-telling book. English thirteenth century, the work of Matthew Paris. MS. Ashmole 304, fol. 31v (detail)" (Derrida 1987: title page verso). The representations of Plato and Socrates are necessarily imaginative reproductions, and even if the illustration does exist as a postcard, it would do so only as a secondary representation of the frontispiece. By the time it is reproduced on the cover of Derrida's text, it is at least twice removed from the original. This question of the model and its imitation replays the investigations of mimesis we saw Derrida map out in *Dissemination*.

Investigating the relationships between doubles (the *je* and the *toi* as well as the *vous* and *tu* in the French version of Derrida's text, and also the double between the desirer and the object of desire), Derrida describes the story of the double ("*Our* story" [emphasis added]) as a "twin progeniture, a procession of Sosie/sosie, Atreus/Thyestes, Shem/Shaun, S/p, p/p (*penman/postman*) and more and more I metempsychose myself from you" (Derrida 1987a:142). From this "procession," Benstock formulates the Derridean principle of writing as a continual production of "doubles": "Writing gives rise to this [metempsychose] of One and Other that drives the pen, that is heard in the dialogue of all writing, so that the writing of letters [Derrida's postcards and the *Wake*'s letters]—the establishment of a correspondence—creates a set of doubles, doubled" (Benstock 1984:173).

Benstock demonstrates how the "double bind" of writing explored and articulated in *The Post Card* is the same double bind produced in the *Wake*. It is the double produced by a mimetic reproduction of a model and that produced by the self that writes to (and for) the object of desire that is simultaneously addressed and reproduced in writing. This double creates the "dialectic of One and Other hypothesized in the setting of pen to paper" (Benstock 1984:173). The double is also subversive because "authority is problematized by the act that would seem to establish (that is, underwrite) authority" (Benstock 1984:173).

In the next chapter, we will examine Derrida's interest in the *Wake*'s narrative of the myth of Babel and his description of Joyce's writing as "babelizing." Benstock's explanation of Derrida's interest in Joyce's retelling of the Babel story (and his "babelizing" writing), argues that the "process of duplication and division [which] best illustrates [the production of the double bind] is the building of the tower of Babel" as it is articulated in the *Wake* (Benstock 1984:173).

After looking at Derrida's use of Joyce's version of the Babel myth, she explains the terms in which Derrida "poses the questions of *Wake* writing" and how these terms are at work in the *Wake:*

(1) the need to authorize a text by signing one's name to it; (2) the demand of the father (*Dieu*, the Master, YHWH, HCE) that one both hear and not hear, both inscribe and hide, his name in the language, a demand that both mandates and erases . . . the translation of his name

through language, a demand that is the *double bind* of all writing; (3) the division between language and that which it describes . . . the necessity of language disseminated and dispersed . . . to fall into the hands of—be translated by—a third party; of necessity, the letter Shem pens is posted through Shaun, following a trajectory that Shaun as carrier rather than Shem as writer determines. (Benstock 1984:174)

Benstock concludes her investigation of Derrida and Joyce with an analysis of the *Wake*'s letters within the frames of writing she finds at work in both writers. The ultimate and inevitable destination for all desire expressed in, and constituted by, writing is death. Until that destination is reached, desire is sustained in a series of displacements and transferences perpetuated by the exchange of writing in correspondence. The ways in which correspondence is delayed, misplaced, or misdirected enable desire to operate until it arrives at its final destination. For Benstock, both the "postal systems of *La Carte Postale* and *Finnegans Wake* illustrate the various ways that the communication of desire can go astray, be lost, be delayed, or transferred" (Benstock 1984:184).

Unlike Shari Benstock, Murray McArthur does not initially examine the possibility that *The Post Card* may be mirroring, rearticulating, and putting back into practice the double bind of Joyce's writing. Instead, he explores Joyce's position in Derrida's text as the "place of the example, exemplar, model or paradigm in Derrida's textual practice" (McArthur 1995:227). Emphasizing Joyce's "necessity" for deconstruction, he begins with the thesis that "Joyce's example of equivocity, his babelization and his condensation of the whole within the part, his condensation of the example down to the very letters, is what makes his project necessary to deconstruction." This is the purpose of "The Example of Joyce: Derrida Reading Joyce": "to read how Derrida has figured that necessity, how he has read Joyce and, as he claims, been read by Joyce" (McArthur 1995:228).

McArthur uses the Joycean figure of the labyrinth to describe the "vast network of imbricated rhetorics and emblematics or relation" in which he sees Joyce operating as Derrida's "example," and he "follows Derrida's own directions" as the "quickest way into, if not out of, this labyrinth." He does not trace Derrida's engagement with Joyce's writing as it unfolds within *The Post Card,* but focuses immediately upon the card describing Derrida's visit to Joyce's statue in the Fluntern Cemetery in Zurich. This card, dated "20 June 1978," describes the cemetery as a "museum of the most costly horrors," and Derrida links the statue of Joyce with Joyce's "reading" of all of his own future readers: "a life-size Joyce, in other words colossal in this place, seated, with his cane, a cigarette in hand it seems to me, and a book in the other hand. He has read all of us—and plundered us, that one. I imagined him looking at himself posed there—by his zealous descendants I suppose" (Derrida 1987a:148).

Derrida then allows for the possibility of chance playing its part in his visit to the cemetery in the same way that he attempts to let it operate in so much of his other writing: "We continued to walk around in the cemetery, speaking, I believe, about Poe and Yale, all that." The "chance" encounter then occurs: "At the end of an alley, the tomb of the inventor of something like the telescripter: Egon Zoller, *Erfinder des Telephonographen*. This inscription is engraved in stone between two globes, one of which bears the Alpha and the Omega, and the other meridians and a kind of telephonic device spitting out a band of paper." This "chance" discovery of an inventor in the field of communications technology from which Derrida often draws his metaphors for Joyce's writing (telephone, telegraph, gramophone, radio, computer) has a comic effect, releasing the repression of the earlier "most costly horrors": "After the raucous burst of laughter we spent a long time musing in front of this phallus of modernity" (Derrida 1987a:148).

McArthur explores Derrida's encounter with Joyce's statue in the context of a Freudian "primal scene." Linking the statue postcard with the cover engraving of Plato and Socrates as the two centers of *The Post Card*, he suggests these two "overlapping centres . . . can be used to read one another, the engraved scene providing the context for the cemetery events" (McArthur 1995:228). The engraving of Plato and Socrates "provides an emblematics of relation and production, of primal scene and principles of selection." More importantly, "other figures can be and are positioned in the place of the two philosophers," and this is what McArthur does, placing Joyce and Derrida in the place of Socrates and Plato: "If Joyce looked at himself with Derrida beside him, he would recognize that he is in the position of Socrates." "Who," he asks, "stands in the place of Plato, in this odd couple of five and sevens, of unleashed reversibility and substitutability? . . . Now, clearly, it is Derrida himself, the philosopher writing philosophy as if it were literature, the writer implicated in all the rhetorics and emblematics of relation with this colossus, as grandson, son, brother, friend, lover, antagonist, legatee" (McArthur 1995:233).

Exploring Derrida's comment about his desire to imitate Joyce—"Never have I imitated anyone so irresistibly" (Derrida 1987a:142)—McArthur concludes that Joyce "both haunts and drives Derrida" and has the same effect on all of Joyce's readers. Derrida is haunted and driven because Joyce preceded him "in his massive exploitation of postal technology, of letters and writing, of sending and receiving, pairing and coupling, of babelizing in the *Wake*," yet Joyce also produces a "reading or plundering of all of us" (McArthur 1995:235).

Drawing on the technique of doubling with which he explores the relationships of Socrates and Plato and Shem and Shaun, Derrida casts himself in the role of Joyce's double, taking Joyce as his "other." The desire to imitate Joyce "so irresistibly" culminates in Derrida's desire to sit on the knees of Joyce's funereal statue and read Joyce's text aloud. Joyce has written the last word: "After him, no more starting over, draw the veil and let everything come to pass behind the curtains of language at the end of its rope. A coincidence nonetheless, for that seminar on translation I followed all the Babelian indications in *Finnegans Wake* and yesterday I wanted to take the plane to Zurich and read out loud sitting on his knees, starting with the beginning (Babel, the fall, and the Finno-Phoenician motif)" (Derrida 1987a:240).

McArthur's study eventually maps out several of the double patterns we have already seen at work in both Joyce and Derrida. Like Benstock, he examines the "twin progeniture" with which Derrida marks the doubling of "Sosie/sosie . . . Shem/Shaun, S/p," and the Socrates/Plato pairing with which Derrida tropes his relationship with Joyce. McArthur notes how the visit to the cemetery in Zurich is doubled by a similar scene in America, where Derrida runs with a friend whose name is a double of Joyce's: "Speaking of cemeteries, I announce to you that I have begun to run with Jim . . . and we run in the big cemetery. Talking all the time, as is correct, and from time to time I stop, panting, next to a tomb . . . Jim takes my pulse (he's marvellous, I'll tell you about Jim, he's a little crazy with his jogging, I don't know what he is settling with it, but in everything and for everything he is a master, I think he knows everything)" (Derrida 1987a:157).

The operations of such doubling enable McArthur to look at how the "twin forces of war and love" function in a "displaced and repressed" guise within the operations of desire, and he draws on Benstock's account of desire's displacement and the repression of war and hate in the *Wake*'s "postal system of desire" (Benstock 1984:163; McArthur 1995:236). The double motivation of desire resulting from its repression and displacement of the forces behind love and war can be traced back to desire's (double) oscillations between the death and reproductive impulses identified by Freud; this is a context that *The Post Card* opens up when Derrida shifts his attentions from the Socrates/Plato, Joyce/Derrida pairings and examines, in "Freud's Legacy" and "Paralysis," the double patterns at work in Freud's analysis of desire.

The patterns of "double motivation" at work in Derrida's engagement with Joyce are "most succinctly demonstrated" in Derrida's use of Joyce's *Giacomo Joyce,* an immensely powerful section of *The Post Card* because it "scans, reads, pillages all the 'envois' [of *The Post Card*] in advance, in reverse." *Giacomo Joyce* "both anticipates and interprets" *The Post Card,* "reading and dictating its codes" (McArthur 1995:237). The postcard dated "11 August 1979" opens and closes with a citation of this text: "James (the two, the three), Jacques, Giacomo Joyce—your *contrefacture* is a marvel, the counterpart to the *invoice: 'Envoy: love me love my umbrella. . . .* I forgot, Giacomo also has seven letters. Love my *ombre, elle*—not me. 'Do you love me?' And you, tell me" (Derrida 1987a:238–39).

Within the context of Derrida's interest in Joyce's "babelization" of language, the moves that Derrida makes as he shifts from "James" through "Giacomo" to his own name, "Jacques," are an example of the double bind of translation (we must not translate, but that is all we can do) examined in more detail by the next chapters. These shifts should be read in the context of "babelization" and the double bind of translation. The passage is "highly babelized" and "virtually impossible to translate." The problem is created by "Giacomo Joyce" being a "babelic name, like *Socrate* and Plato": it is "one of the hundred words of seven and five letters" (McArthur 1995:237). In "Two Words for Joyce," Derrida underlines the importance of *Giacomo Joyce* for *The Post Card,* a text that is "[a]bove all . . . haunted by Joyce": "With a whole family of James, Jacques, Giacomo, the *Giacomo Joyce* scans all the *Envois* which are sealed, near the end, by the *Envoy* of G.C." (Derrida 1984a:151). Derrida follows this with a recitation of the passages from *Giacomo Joyce* we have just examined.

In an interview with Derek Attridge examined in the next chapter, Derrida explains how he sees writing involved in another version of the double structure. As a writer responds to a text that he has read, it is not possible to separate this textual response from an autobiographical response. The reading of texts in which Derrida "mark[s] out and read[s] a text simultaneously almost identical and entirely other" is both an autobiographical response and, at the same time, a textual response (Derrida 1987b:4). The separation of the two is an artificial separation that must feign to distinguish between the two while recognizing that such a separation is ultimately impossible.

Discussing how his "adolescent desire" "directed [him] towards something in writing which was neither" literature nor philosophy, Derrida suggests that "'[a]utobiography' is perhaps the least inadequate name, because it remains for me the most enigmatic, the most open, even today" (Derrida 1992b:34). This desire is itself autobiographic and manifests the same double structures of desire in general and of writing structured by desire: "the desire to write came to me . . . in a way that was *as obscure as it was compulsive, both powerless and authoritarian*" (Derrida 1992b:34; emphasis added).

McArthur suggests that it is just such a double structure and autobiographical element that makes *Giacomo Joyce* so important to *The Post Card* and that Joyce's text "both anticipates and interprets the later text, reading and dictating its codes." While *Giacomo Joyce* was published posthumously, it began, like *The Post Card,* "as a private love offering, whose addressee is both known and unknown, hidden in code" (McArthur 1995:237). McArthur identifies Joyce's student, Amalia Popper, as the addressee of *Giacomo Joyce* (McArthur 1995:241 n. 14). He then maps out the ways in which Derrida's *envois,* or postcards, are encoded and structured by the codes and patterns of Joyce's text.

Both texts hesitate "between private and public, pulling back, in [Joyce's] case into the private." Both texts are also "generically uncertain, both autobiographical and fictional, both continuous and discontinuous, both open and closed" (McArthur 1995:237). Both texts thus work against the traditional structure of the book in similar ways to other writings by Joyce and Derrida. Like Derrida's text, Joyce's has a double structure with which it simultaneously "shows and hides its principles of selection"; its "entries begin and end and are arranged according to a code that may only be known to the author" (McArthur 1995:237). The "notion of [such] a personal, hidden code is reinforced" by the ways in which both *The Post Card* and *Giacomo Joyce* contain textual "fragments" that appear in the writers' other texts (McArthur 1995:237).

McArthur situates Derrida's reading of Joyce and the ways in which *The Post Card* is read in advance by Joyce's writings in the context of Joyce's achievement of a dream in which all of his readers must take part. In the establishment of literary institutions (the International James Joyce Foundation, the Bailey's Annual James Joyce Summer School, the *JJQ,* the *James Joyce Literary Supplement,* the foundations and various organizations bearing Joyce's name in Zurich, Miami, Tokyo, Sydney, England) devoted to his work, Joyce has attained his dream of "a special institution for his oeuvre, inaugurated by it like a new order." For Derrida, this achievement means

that we are all "people or characters in part constituted (as readers, writers, critics, teachers) *in* and *through* Joyce's dream. Aren't we Joyce's dream, his dream readers, the ones he dreamed of and whom we dream of being in our turn?" (Derrida 1992b:74).

It is the powerful irruption of this dream and its double effects within the history of the deconstructive operations of writing that Derrida marks out in his engagements with Joyce. While confessing his "intimidation" by Joyce scholars and admitting that "incompetence" is the "profound truth of [his] relationship to [Joyce's] work," Derrida simultaneously contends that "there can be no Joycean competence, in the certain and strict sense of the concept of competence" (Derrida 1992a:280, 282).

The irony at work in Derrida's double position (he is "incompetent" in a field in which there can be no competence) re-marks the "sort of irony" that "ultimately all literary rhetoric in general" practices in its deconstructive phases. Agreeing with Paul de Man's suggestion that all such rhetoric "is of itself deconstructive," Derrida argues that "an irony of detachment" is at work "with regard to metaphysical belief or thesis, even when it apparently puts it forward" (Derrida 1992b:50).

CHAPTER 5

Example and Counterexample

Finnegans Wake **and** *Glas*

CHRISTOPHER NORRIS DESCRIBES *Glas*
as "Joycean," a description that Geoffrey Bennington labels "silly" (Norris
1987:243; Bennington 1994:18). There is, however, a set of relationships to
be articulated between the two texts that Derrida himself has acknowledged
in calling *Glas* "a sort of wake" (Derrida 1984a:150). *Glas* focuses on the
work of Hegel and Genet, and the possibility we have already seen Derrida
consider—that Joyce may be the "most Hegelian of novelists"—is worth
keeping in mind while examining how Derrida countersigns Joyce's techniques with *Glas*. At the level of the text's overall structure, Derrida's writing deconstructs the form in which that writing is presented in ways that
continue his investigation of such notions as presence, existence, unity, and
mimesis as they are articulated in language. He interrogates the conceptual
horizons of the literary and philosophical discourse exploited in *Glas*.

It is in "Two Words for Joyce" that Derrida describes *Glas* as "also a sort
of wake." While there is no apparent direct reference to Joyce's writing in

Glas, "Two Words for Joyce" makes it clear that Derrida is playfully alluding to Joyce's text with his use of the term *wake*. There are numerous textual and thematic similarities between *Finnegans Wake* and *Glas,* and it is clear that his reading of Joyce's text haunts the ways in which Derrida has constructed his exploration of Hegel and Genet by positioning separate and discrete textual columns next to each other so that it is necessary to read intertextually and follow the ways in which the textual play operates across and between the margins or borders of the page(s) and space(s) separating the columns.

Both Joyce's text and Derrida's engage with the seminal question of the relationship of writing and (inherited) religion. In *Glas* Derrida returns to the complex issue of Judaism (at work in the essay on Levinas and explored again in "Two Words for Joyce") in an exploration of Hegel's meditation on Jewish history and the Jewish family as well as in the motif of circumcision, which Derrida explores as a "simulacrum of castration" in the writing of Genet. The two words in "Two Words for Joyce" are *He war;* we have seen Derrida analyze Joyce's pun on "war" and "true" (Ger. *wahr*) in order to read *HEWAR* as an anagram of YAHWE, the Jewish God who proclaims, "I am he who is or who am," and who declares war on humankind: "He war: he was—he who was. . . . Where it was, he was, declaring war, and it is *true*" (Derrida 1984a:145).

Susan Handelman has explored Derrida's relationship with Hebraism. She defines the alterity of Derrida's position in relationship to rabbinical thought. Derrida's is a "heretic hermeneutic," and the "specific form" of his Jewish heresy is "metonymy run amok," a metonymy "declaring itself to be independent of all foundations and yet claiming to be the origin and law of everything" (Handelman 1982:122). One of the great attractions of the *Wake* for Derrida is Joyce's version of this "mad" metonymy and the metonymic chains that sustain the many puns on which the *Wake* is founded.

Joyce's importance in Derrida's work is also explained by the high stakes played for by both of these religious exiles. Joyce thought of the *Wake* in biblical terms, revealing this in the well-known defense of his use of punning, wherein he compares the puns on which the *Wake* is founded with the foundation of Christianity: "The Holy Roman Catholic Apostolic Church was built on a pun. It ought to be good enough for me" (Ellmann 1983:546). Handelman has shown that in addition to being "also a sort of a wake" modeled on Joyce's text, *Glas* follows the intertextual model of the Talmud, whose "central pattern of the text surrounded by commentary" is "also the format of Derrida's *Glas*" (Handelman 1982:47). What is at stake, in both texts, for both writers, is the configuration of the relationship of word and Word and of all that this relationship entails.

The three *Wake*an techniques foregrounded in *Glas* are: (1) a radical exploitation of paronomasia, (2) the use of a circular structure for the text, and (3) the construction of pages from columns and marginalia engaged in a textual interplay like that of the Talmud and the intertextual structure Joyce constructed for section 11.2 of the *Wake*. The importance of Derrida's use of a Joyceanlike paronomasia is echoed in Geoffrey Hartman's *Saving the Text* and particularly in "Epiphony in Echoland" (Hartman 1981:33–66).

Hartman reads the word *Glas* as a pun on the final syllables of the French pronunciation of Hegel and *aigle,* attesting to Derrida's following of the Joycean paronomasian inscription of desire and death: *Glas* is an onomatopoeic "sound word" that "refers to the death knell or passing bell." The word is "endlessly '*joyced*' by [Derrida], to suggest that voice has no monument except in the form of a rattle in the throat covered or sublimed by the passing bell" (Hartman 1981:5; my emphasis). Hartman uses Joyce's name as a verb to refer to Derrida's use of Joyce's paronomasia, but *joycing* is also a usefully playful term for Derrida's adaptation of the *Wake*'s circularity as well as his adaptation of the intertextual play of the *Wake*'s lessons section.

Bennington disagrees with Hartman's reading of *Glas*. He uses Derrida's statement that there is "not one single pun" in *Glas* to describe *Joycean* as a "silly" adjective for the text. He does not explore the possibility that Derrida's statement may be ironic, or the fact that Derrida's writings, like those of Joyce, reveal that no pun is ever "single": all puns entail at least a double phonetic relationship (even when this phonetic relationship is realized graphically as it frequently is with the GL in *Glas*) with at least one other word (in Joyce's case the relationships are frequently more than double as Joyce's is an overdetermined paronomasia) (Bennington 1994: 18). Puns and homonyms proliferate in *Glas: voleur* (Fr., "steal") and *volens* (Lat., "willing," a pun which also reproduces Joyce's pun, *nolens volens* [Derrida 1986a:171; *FW* 271.20]); the extended puns on *coup* (cut and blow), *coud* (sew), *cou* (neck), *cul* (ass), *col* (collar), and *colle* (glue) (Derrida 1986a:162, 169, 179), and the circular and extremely *Wake*an series of numerous puns (*Gallia, Gallien, Gallows galalith, galley,* and *galactic* (Derrida 1986a:121–24, *passim*) generated from the GL of *Glas* practices the same textual generation and proliferation as Joyce's production of phrases and names from HCE and ALP.

Derrida stresses the importance of the joycing, or Joyceanlike, punning of *Glas* in his introduction to John P. Leavey Jr.'s *Glassary* for *Glas,* "Proverb: 'He that would pun'." These four words echo those of "Two Words for Joyce," and Derrida sustains this echoing effect in repeating "two words" as he states: "I shall say then *two words.* Just *two words,* and of unequal length . . . I limit myself to two English words: *edition* and *pun*" (Derrida 1986b:17; emphasis added). Punning on the word *paronomasia* and the Greek *para-nomos,* Derrida suggests that puns may be *para nomos,* or "against the law," and that "the pun must be morally condemned and as such proscribed, for the pun signals some malice . . . a perverse tendency to transgress the laws of society" (Derrida 1986b:18).

In the same way that the *Wake*'s puns work in part to undermine certain traditional, established literary conventions (for example, that plots have a clear and well-made, tripartite, beginning-middle-end pattern; that characters be clearly named and recognizable as separate and individual characters), Derrida's puns are a part of his attempt to ensure that *Glas* "remains illegible to the extent that it is performed in the literary mode of singularity, rather than in the academic mode of conformity."

This "mode of singularity" re-marks Derrida's indebtedness to what he terms the "singular event of Joyce's work" (Derrida 1984a:146). Because Joyce's singularity "both orders and forbids translation" (Derrida 1984a: 154) his work cannot be readily received into academies that concern themselves with translation (of one language into another, of the language of literature into the language of commentary, of the pun into its component terms, and, most importantly for Derrida, of literature into philosophy or vice versa). Derrida believes that "by introducing the unreceivable into the discourse of the academy a powerful effect may take place, assisting more effectively than would a rationally organized persuasion, a change in reading, making possible a previously unheard of reading" (Leavey 1986: 113c, b).

In the same way that the *Wake*'s circular textuality evades the conventional notion of a linear book with a traditional beginning, middle, and end, the circular structure of *Glas* reveals Derrida's attempt to break with the conventional academic structure of a philosophical text. (And, it should be noted, both the conventional notions of the book and the traditional academic structure of the philosophical text "mimic" the linearity of Judaic and Christian teleology.) *Glas* is "not composed in the conventional manner of the academic book because it is explicitly an anti-book, written as an alternative to the classical model of the book" (Leavey 1986:29c).

Opening up the question of the double structure, *Glas* aligns the attempt at producing a linear text with a certain "silliness": "But if I linearize, if I line myself up and believe—silliness—that I write only one text at a time, that comes back to the same thing, and the cost of the margin must still be reckoned with. I win and I lose, in every case, my prick" (Derrida 1986a:66). Retracing the network of themes on the prick in Genet's writing, Derrida opens a series of metaphors on the prick as the pen, the penis, the stylus, and the inscription with which the pen pricks the paper in the process of linear inscription. This is one part of the "double posture" inscribed in the margins of the passage on linearization and the prick.

The "other" of the prick in the "double posture" is troped as the circle that can enfold the prick and invaginate it. The metaphor is again double: both sexual and textual, linking writing with the operations of desire: "Double postulation. Contradiction in (it)self of two irreconcilable desires. Here I give it, accused in my own tongue, the title DOUBLE BAND(S), putting it (them) into form and into play practically. A text laces [sangle] in two senses, in two senses, in two directions. Twice girt. Band contra band" (Derrida 1986a:66). The other side of linearity and of the prick (and the "other" of the desire making the prick erect), their double, are the circle and "band" that Derrida tropes as a "necklace," a "golden fleece," and a "cunt."

Using the metaphor of the spine of the book as a phallic column, as the "other" of the circular flow of language within the text, the *Wake*'s invitation to join the last and first pages of its printed text can be read as the invitation to allow the flowing of ALP's "riverrun" language to encircle and enclose the spine bearing the masculine title of the book in precisely the sort of lacing identified by Derrida.

Tracing Genet's metaphors in *Miracle of the Rose,* Derrida remarks how the "Golden Fleece" "necklace" marks the ring of decapitation, "assign[s] to the executioner the parting line (circumcision or castration)" (Derrida 1986a:62). It marks (by covering) both the neck joining head to body and the severance of head from body, both erection and castration: "The golden fleece surrounds the neck, the cunt, the verge, the apparition or the appearance of a hole in erection, of a hole and an erection at once . . . the fleece surrounds a volcano" (Derrida 1986a:66).

The *Wake*'s lessons section tropes HCE and ALP as Joyce's version of the prick and the cunt: "this upright one, with that noughty besighed him zeroine" (*FW* 261.23–24). The sexual signification of the "upright one" and the "noughty" is triggered by the pun on *nought* and *naughty* at work in "noughty." At a fundamental physical level, the "upright one" and the "noughty" are mathematical—1 and 0—and textual—HCE's erect penis and ALP's vagina; however, the "noughty" that "besighed" (bespoke, gave

breath to) "him," also making him "zeroine" (zero *ein* [G. "one"] or noth-
ing/one), presents us with another double bind: the erection that is a hole. In
this section, Dolph fulfills both his own desire and that of his brother, Kev,
by using a pencil to draw and establish (erect) the diagram of ALP's vagina.
The sexual implications of the pen as penis are confirmed by the description
of the pen/penis as "a poke stiff" and Issy's comment on "[t]he impudence
of that in girl's things!" (296.29–30 and n. 5). Despite, or perhaps because
of, the "impudence" of "that," the pencil line of desire and the diagram of
the desired are a "[d]ouble postulation," a "[c]ontradiction in (it)self of two
irreconcilable desires."

The metaphors of the penis and vagina, or prick and cunt (or the "upright one" and the "noughty"), for the linear and circular, double bind of
the text (its circularity and its upright, phallic, external spine and internal
columns) articulated by the *Wake* find their rearticulation in Derrida's tracing of the same metaphors in his reading of Genet. Derrida uses Genet's
metaphor of the flower-as-glove to explore the operations of this sexual
double bind. The flower, which is "[a]lways to be cut—cuttable—culpable
[*coupable*]" . . . "equals castration, phallus." Simultaneously, it "'signifies'—again!—at least overlaps virginity in general, the vagina, the clitoris,
'feminine sexuality,' matrilinear genealogy" (Derrida 1986a:17, 47).

At stake in this flower metaphor are the simultaneity and equivalence of
double structures. These are troped as the simultaneity and equivalence of
the castration/phallus and the hymen/vagina. "For castration to overlap
virginity, for the phallus to be reversed into the vagina, for alleged opposites
to be equivalent to each other, . . . the flower has to be turned inside out like
a glove, and its style like a sheath" (Derrida 1986a:47). This "*Glove* is
stretched as a signifier of artifice." It is a metaphor for flowers, for the
flowering of desire (as well as the simultaneously other of flowering: the
deflowering of [de]siring) and for the ways in which the phallus can be
"reversed into the vagina."

This floral and sexual (flowering and deflowering mark the duality of
desire's operations) metaphor operates across the borders at the foundational distinction between nature and culture or the natural and the artificial. The expression of desire with what the *Wake* terms "all flores of
speech" (*FW* 143.04) brings the forces of natural desire within the artifice
of culture, releasing and realizing them within the play of a language that
feigns to represent this desire while operating as its simulacra. The 1 and 0
of HCE and ALP, which are both mathematical signifiers and what *Glas*
terms the "prick" and the "cunt," are set to work as signifiers that transcend

the limitations of the "vulgar" code, which would align them only with male and female genitalia (in *Glas,* according to a double, punning, Joycean/Derridean logic, they can be aligned with "Genetalia"). Their double, feigning significations of numbers and sexual organs operate as fakes while simultaneously participating in the creation of the larger context of linearity and circularity that sustain, at the structural level, the same double binds traced by both Joyce and Derrida.

Reading Genet's *The Maids,* Derrida pursues the logic of the flower/glove knot: "But these gloves are not only artificial and reversible signifiers, they are almost fake gloves, kitchen gloves, the 'dish-gloves' with which . . . the strangling of Madame is mimed. . . . *The Maids* are gloves, the gloves of Madame. . . . [a]t once castrated and castrating . . . full and void of the phallus of Madame that Madame does not have" (Derrida 1986a:47–48). We should note how, across the page, on the other side of this reading of *The Maids,* the left-hand column offers a discussion, via Hegel, of the logic of the apotropaic: "the Jew effects (on) himself a simulacrum of castration in order to mark his own-ness, his proper-ness. . . . castrating oneself *already,* always already, in order to be able to castrate and repress the threat of castration, renouncing life and mastery in order to secure them . . . losing in advance what one wants to erect; suspending what one raises; *aufheben*" (Derrida 1986a:46). The foreskin and the reversible glove operate between the text signed by Hegel and that by Genet, and the same signifiers open into the *Wake*'s haunting of *Glas.*

In *Finnegans Wake,* the metaphors of the foreskin and the reversible glove operate as ALP simultaneously draws HCE into her "languo of flows" (as addressee, as the subject of her language, and the one who is both penetrating and penetrated) and invites him to "Rise up" (*FW* 619.25) physically and sexually. ALP is HCE's "elicitous bribe" (*FW* 622.3), or bride, and she "elicit[s]" him to "Reach down. A lil mo. So. Draw back your glave" (*FW* 621.24). "Glave" is an Old-English term for smooth and a term for flattery (*OED*), but it also puns on the "glove" of HCE's foreskin, or "falskin" (*FW* 621.25). When it is drawn back, or reversed, HCE's "Hot and hairy hugon" (his hand and penis) reveals a head that is "Smoos as an infams" (*FW* 621.25–26).

The glove/"falskin" reversing to reveal the qualities of both infancy and infamy ("infams") is also involved in suggestions of castration and duplicitous doubling: "One time you told you'd been burnt in ice. And one time it was chemicalled after you taking a lifeness. Maybe that's why you hold your hodd as if. And people thinks you missed the scaffold. Of fell design"

(*FW* 621.26–29). "[T]aking a lifeness," "hold[ing] your hod as if," leaving "people" to think that "you missed the scaffold": modes of "suspending what one raises."

The "double posture" which is also a double bind, (con)fusing linearity and circulation, is enacted graphically on the pages of both *Glas* and the *Wake*. The ways in which the *Wake*'s final and opening words (in terms of physical placement) could be joined together to defeat the traditional closure of the book's physical and material beginning and closing are replayed by the double columns of *Glas*. The left-hand column on the final page of the text ends with the words "But it runs to its ruin [*perte*], for it counted without [*sans*]" (Derrida 1986a:262). As in the *Wake,* there is no final punctuation mark to this concluding, incomplete sentence, and the opening words of *Glas* provide a predicate to follow the preposition "without [*sans*]": "what, after all, of the remain(s), today, for us, here, now of a Hegel?" (Derrida 1986a:1).

Similarly, the final words in the right-hand column of *Glas* are: "Today, here, now, the debris of [*débris de*]" (Derrida 1986a:262). This sentence fragment also lacks any final punctuation mark and can be linked, via the lowercased (uncapitalized), initial word of *Glas*'s opening right-hand column, with: "*what remained of a Rembrandt torn into small, very regular squares and rammed down the shithole* is divided in two" (Derrida 1986a:1).

The structure of the first sentence is such that it fuses together an assertion ("But it runs to its ruin [*perte*]"); a causal assertion ("But it runs to its ruin [*perte*], *for it counted*" [emphasis added]); and at least two questions ("But it runs to its ruin [*perte*], for it counted without [*sans*]," "what, after all"? *and* "what, after all . . . remain(s), today, for us, here, now, of a Hegel?"). This (con)fusion of assertion and answer repeats a similar (con)fusion to that of the initial sentence of the *Wake*'s lessons section: "As we there are where are we are we there from tomtittot to teetootomtotalitarian" (*FW* 260.1–2). This sentence can be broken down into the assertions "we there are" and questions like "where are we?" and "are we there?."

The structure of the two sentences working across the gap between the closing and initial pages of *Glas* is such that it is possible to join the ultimate words of the left-hand column with the initial words of the right-hand column and vice versa. This possibility is supported by Derrida's comments on the chiasmus at work throughout *Glas:* "X, an almost perfect chiasm-(us), more than perfect, of the two texts, each one set facing [*en regard*] the other: a gallery and a graphy that guard one another and disappear from view." Derrida describes how the chiasmus leads the reader from one column to another: "The word 'regard' that opens the right column fixes you again at the end of the left column" (Derrida 1986a:43–44).

The alternative, chiastic structure for the two sentences to be linked by the reader would be as follows:

(Closing L-hand) "But it runs to its ruin [*perte*], for it counted without [*sans*]" (Opening R-hand) "*what remained of a Rembrandt torn into small, very regular squares and rammed down the shithole*' is divided in two."

(Closing R-hand) "Today, here now, the debris of [*debris de*]" (Opening L-hand) "what, after all, of the remain(s), today, for us, here, now, of a Hegel?"

The themes of ruin and survival, the relationships between history and the present and art and philosophy restage Derrida's earlier concerns with these themes in his use of Joyce's project as a counter for Husserl's phenomenology. The consolidation of empirical history can threaten the ideal forms Husserl sought by concealing and ruining them with equivocal forms of language, making it impossible to articulate their pure forms in the present. Joyce's literary equivocal project operates as the double of Husserl's philosophical struggle for univocity. Joyce's art strives to escape from history by displaying it in the presence of a complete equivocity; Husserl's philosophy attempts to purify history of equivocity in order to grasp the historical forms of the ideal at their origin.

Glas's investigation of Hegel's philosophy and Genet's art is interwoven with the themes of ruin and survival sustained in both columns. Linking the columns by reading them as continuations of each other in the double reading made possible by the "Joycing," "Doublends" pattern opens a new, double perspective on these topics and themes, producing a chiastic link between them. This chiastic crossover also reproduces some of the effects created by the crossing over of the left-and right-hand marginal comments in the *Wake*'s lessons section.

Derrida's willingness to introduce "unreceivable" (by academia) writing practices (including puns, double structures [of texts, of words, of letters, of punctuation marks and parentheses], "non-concepts") into his philosophical discourse and his interest in allowing literature (and, most importantly here, the writings of Joyce) to "contaminate" his philosophical work enables his writing to avoid the limiting "fixing [of] a mission" for either literature or philosophy at the same time that it enables him to interrogate the essence of literature and practice a philosophy that "interrogate[s] the relationship between speech and writing" (Derrida 1992a:38–39).

The rational and regulated analytic methods of academic discourse can explain the effects of the pun, but in so doing they leave no room for it to operate:

> As soon as, in one mode or another, actually or virtually, one analyses, exposes, and so demonstrates rules of deformation, condensation, displacement, the new glossary and the new grammar no longer leave any place for the *pun,* at least if . . . one persists in understanding by this word, as is often done in certain socio-ideological situations and to defend certain norms, the free play, the complacent and slightly narcissistic relation to language, the exercise of virtuosity to no profit, without economy of sense or knowledge, without any necessity but that of enjoying one's mastery over one's language and the others. (Derrida 1986b:18a)

A significant part of Derrida's engagement with the puns and babelizing of Joyce's "babbling" language is a result of his interest in his own Hebraic background and his interest in sacred Hebraic texts. We have already touched on Derrida's concern with Judaism and his use of Joyce's proposition ("Jewgreek is greekjew. Extremes meet") in his reading of Levinas, as well as the importance of Derrida's Judaism in the "Circumfessions" of *Jacques Derrida.* Joyce's use of the Babel myth—a use Derrida emphasizes in "Two Words for Joyce"—is an important part of the *Wake*'s status as an ersatz of a sacred book such as the Bible. This helps to account for the recurring motif of the biblical narrative of the tower of Babel in Joyce's text, a motif to which Derrida returns in his discussions of Joyce. Susan Handelman has conducted extensive investigations into the general similarities between Derrida's concept of *écriture* and the traditions of Hebraic sacred writings and noted the similar typographical arrangements between those writings and *Glas* (Handelman 1982).

Her study shows how the marginal annotations and exegeses become incorporated as a part of the sacred text to which they refer and on which they comment. There is, then, an "academic" precedent to Derrida's practice. At the same time, the arrangement of the text on the pages of *Glas* is similar to the *Wake*'s lessons section and provokes a similar double and chiastic reading of the text. It is possible to see *Glas* as a playing out of the "literary" possibilities (of both theological and philosophical texts) in the "academic" mode.

Glas is not the only text in which Derrida has set to work the typographical patterns found in both the Talmud and the *Wake.* At the beginning of

"The Double Session" in *Dissemination*, for example, he lays out two discrete sections of text on one page. The first twelve lines consist of a citation of *Philebus* in which Socrates and Protarchus discuss some of the relationships among thought, speech, and writing (Plato 1961:1118e–1119c). After these initial twelve lines, the page is vertically divided into two parts, and a passage from Mallarmé's *Mimique* is set alongside the rest of the passage from *Philebus*. At the point where the page is divided into two columns, Socrates and Protarchus have moved on to the theme of painting. This theme is echoed by Mallarmé's meditations on the metaphor of an orchestra "marking with its gold, its brushes with thought and dusk" (Derrida 1981:175). Derrida sets these two pieces together for several purposes. These include: a re-marking of the historical periods between Plato's classical Greek thought and Mallarmé's modernism; an echoing of Socrates' discussion of language and painting by Mallarmé's thoughts on silence and the character of Pierrot; and an opening up of the relationships between philosophy and literature that Derrida uses as the "double bottom" for the investigation of mimesis that dominates much of *Dissemination*.

The placing together of different, discrete sections of text is more complex in *Glas* than it is in "The Double Session." In *Glas*, citations from Hegel and Genet are interspersed with Derrida's own comments and citations from other texts, both of which explain, echo, and/or amplify the topics of literature, philosophy, and writing; the themes of ruin and survival, of desire, femininity, and masculinity, of sexuality, domesticity and death; and motifs and images of invagination and ensheathing, of penetration and inscription, and of circumcision, castration and production that are simultaneously at work in the citations of Hegel and Genet. For the most part, the pages of *Glas* are laid out in either two or three columns organized in such a way that the reading of one column simultaneously contaminates and illuminates the reading of its partner(s). On some pages, small blocks of text are grafted into one or more of the major columns in such a way as to interrupt the development of the major column while simultaneously commenting upon it.

What is foregrounded in the *Wake*'s lessons section, "The Double Session," and *Glas* is the successful creation of "bifurcated writing" and the sort of "grouped textual field" that is the only site, Derrida argues, in which a deconstructive overturning of classical philosophical hierarchies can "be marked" (Derrida 1987b:41–42). While many of Derrida's texts reveal such double and bifurcated inscriptions, "The Double Session" and *Glas*, like Joyce's lessons section, foreground and draw attention to this writing through similar typographical arrangements and layouts on their pages.

Derrida contends that the operations of deconstruction are "impossible to point . . . out, for a unilinear text, or a punctual *position,* an operation signed by a single author" (Derrida 1987b:42). He has constructed his grouped textual fields from texts "signed" by Plato, Mallarmé, Hegel, Genet, Joyce, and so on. Joyce's lessons section feigns a signing by the fictional characters of Shem, Shaun, and Issy, but it also includes the fragment "signed" by Quinet and the double intertwined circles of the *vesica piscis,* which must have been "signed" by numerous writers and artists before Dolph added his own signature to the list. (We should also note that the marginal annotations and exegeses of Hebraic sacred writings are "signed" by or credited to various Rabbis.)

Shari Benstock's investigation of Joyce's lessons section pinpoints some of the specific ways in which the columns of that section operate deconstructively. "At the Margins of Discourse: Footnotes in the Fictional Text" offers a close analysis of how the footnotes of the lessons section produce a "subvention of . . . authorial prerogative" (Benstock 1983:211). These footnotes are more like discrete texts in a deconstructive "grouped textual field" (Derrida 1987b:42) than the footnotes found in scholarly texts. They "do not keep the text within its boundaries, locked into its narrative form; they insist on taking it always 'out of bounds,' taking the reader with them. They resist the very authority they purportedly serve" (Benstock 1983:212).

In the *Wake*'s "NIGHTLETTER" it is the authority of the phallic column dominated by tales of the patriarchal HCE that is resisted and overturned by the female desire of ALP and Issy as well as by the brothers who sustain their desire for the maternal ALP. Derrida's *Glas* "works over phallogocentrism from the side of the mother and of woman." It "follows the law of woman: 'Natural, divine, feminine, nocturnal, familial . . . [i]n this . . . place, of the family" (Leavey 1986:113). Joyce's lessons section has already done precisely the same. The margins and footnotes are the textual sites and positions of the twins and their sister, together creating a "family place." The dialogue of the twins creates the space within the phallogocentric column in which the maternal ALP's diagram is inscribed. In the lessons section, the "upright one" and the paternal "Pep" are worked over "from the side of" the female "noughty" and "Memmy" as well as the familial side of the maternal, the twins and their sister. This family scene is a site of love and romance but also the site of their doubles: warfare and death.

Derrida frequently focuses upon writing as a kind of warfare, and there is a warfare between the discrete textual groups in the lessons section that proceeds as follows: there is an initial intrusion of Issy's text into the space that was previously occupied by the central column (279); the central column responds, as it were, with a retaliatory occupation of Issy's space (280); Shaun's right-hand comments join in the assault with an incursion into the space of the central column (281, 282), before disappearing for three pages (283–85); they fight back with another intrusion into the central area (286), which provokes the central column to expand and take up both marginal spaces for more than five pages (287–92). It then looks as if peace has been restored, until the final page of the section, when the central column is reduced to a "thin" recitation of the numbers one through ten (the number of the section and of the phallic "upright one . . . with that noughty besighed him zeroine" [FW 261.23–24]). The section concludes with the "NIGHT-LETTER" signed by the siblings invading and occupying the space of the central column.

Within the larger context of the Wake's liquid "languo of flows" this invasion is supported by Joyce's own working over of phallogocentric patterns from the side of the mother and the female. ALP is the maternal and dominant female of the narrative, but ALP also signifies the Wake's language. Issy learns woman's writing, or "gramma's grammar" (FW 268.17) from ALP's mother, or Issy's grandmother (her "gramma"), and her language is a part of Anna's writing, the many anagrams Joyce creates functioning as Anna's *grammes*, or written marks.

ALP's name is an important part of Joyce's female working over of phallogocentrism. It can be read as a tightly compressed history of Western languages as those languages swing on what Barbara Johnson calls the "crucial hinges of Western philosophy: the textual rifts and drifts produced by the process of *translation* of the Greek philosophers, precisely, into Latin" (Johnson 1981:182 n. 10). The classical Greek *ana* is a contraction of *anastethi*, or "up! arise!" (Liddell and Scott), and ALP's call for HCE is "*Away! Rise up,* man of the hooths" (FW 619.25, emphasis added). Livia is the feminine declension of the Roman family name, "Livius," and "plurabelle" fuses the modern French *plu, belle, elle,* and *le* with the Latin combining prefix *plura*. It is the woman's language of ALP calling HCE to his resurrection, and Joyce's word is made in female flesh, the biblical god "who is and who was and who is to come" (*Rev.* 1.8) being reworked into the female "Anna was, Livia is, Plurabelle's to be" (FW 215.24).

It is possible, then, to mark Joyce and Derrida's sharing and exploration of similar themes (writing as warfare and patricide; the role and power of the mother and of the attachment to the maternal and familial; the failure and/or death of the phallus; the distinctions between nature and culture as well as those between philosophy and literature; and so on) even if it is not possible to summarize, or "point out," all the effects of such sharing in a unilinear writing such as this.

One can identify the similar textual operations and typographical layouts foregrounded by both writers as they graft together various citations into an intertext. The styles of both writers, however, produce effects that the unilinear writing required and produced by academic and scholarly institutions cannot "point out." Neither writer produces "books" (and this becomes particularly true for Joyce with the *Wake*) in the academic sense of the term, and what Derrida and Leavey say of *Glas* can, in general terms, also be applied to the *Wake:* "it is a 'reading effect' [rather than a book]—an experiment in producing an entirely unanticipated reading . . . The aspect . . . most likely to provoke the defence mechanisms of the institution is its style, which is in any case that which . . . 'remains illegible' to the extent that it is performed in the literary mode of singularity rather than in the academic mode of conformity" (Leavey 1986:113).

Derrida does not claim to have "read" Joyce or to have "proposed a general reading of [his] texts." His interest lies elsewhere: in the "singularity" of Joyce's work, a singularity to which Derrida "tries to respond" or "countersign." Joyce's is an example of an equivocal writing against a limiting historicity and a reductive empiricism. Following his own "'logic' of singularity," Derrida uses Joyce as a "counterexample" of equivocity against the example of Husserl's phenomenological historicism. In *Glas* Derrida "countersigns" his name to the style of Joyce's paronomasia as an "other" name for "he who would pun," echoing, as he does so, the title of his own "two words" for Joyce: "He *war.*"

CHAPTER 6

Speaking of Joyce (I)

The Specter of Joyce in Derrida's Voice(s)

DERRIDA HAS SPOKEN ON JOYCE ON AT
least three occasions. This chapter focuses on the first two of these events,
wherein Derrida spoke primarily on Joyce's texts. In the third of Derrida's
talks, "'This Strange Institution Called Literature': An Interview with Jacques
Derrida," Derrida spoke on Joyce within the context of the relationships
among deconstruction and literature, philosophy, and feminism. This general discussion uses Joyce as a touchstone for what Derrida has to say on
these issues. The next chapter examines it in detail and explores some of the
implications that Derrida's readings of Joyce have for his thoughts on these
matters.

Each time Derrida has spoken on Joyce, Joyce's writings operated within
what Derrida had to say about those writings, even when Derrida's own
spoken words were read from a *written* text. These textual specters of
Joyce's words have important implications for Derrida's investigations of
the relationships between speech and writing and his deconstructive overturning of the classical hierarchy privileging speech over writing.

The privileging of speech over writing is not an isolated event but part of a historical and philosophical textual play occurring between other signifiers attached to each of these terms. In the system of binary opposition, the opposing terms are mutually exclusive: *absence,* for example, is the *complete* or *total* opposite to presence. Attached to speech are signifiers such as presence, goodness, truth, light, male, mastery, and wisdom; attached to writing are absence, badness or evil, falsity, dark, female, enslavement, and foolishness. The double strategy of deconstruction entails marking the interval between the opposing members of each pair from these terms and then reinscribing each of the terms in a new writing practice that "*simultaneously* provokes the overturning of the hierarchy speech/writing, and the entire system attached to it, *and* releases the dissonance of writing within speech" (Derrida 1981:42).

Derrida's speaking on Joyce exemplifies his project of deconstructing the speech/writing hierarchy as it releases the dissonance of Joyce's "writing within [Derrida's] speech." It also reveals a marked change in Derrida's attitude toward Joyce's writing. In the texts examined so far, Derrida uses Joyce's writing, in part, as models and exemplars for the organization of his own texts and as countersignings or counterexamples of Joyce writings. Drawing on many of the motifs, themes, and mythemes articulated by Joyce, Derrida grafts fragments from Joyce's writing into his own so that his double writing can respond to the fragments of Joyce's texts while simultaneously allowing them to signify back toward the site of their removal. In *speaking* on Joyce, however, Derrida reveals a familiarity with Joyce's writing; one effect of which is an increase of the ironic force in his written and stated reluctance to write or speak on Joyce.

If, as McArthur suggests, the depiction of Plato and Socrates from *The Postcard* can be read as a configuration of Joyce and Derrida, then Derrida's talking on Joyce may well suggest that in addition to allowing Joyce's writing to work within his own speech, Derrida has also deconstructively overturned his own relationship to Joyce so that it is no longer a master/disciple relationship, but one in which the student challenges the suppositions of the master and assumes the master's position, containing and regulating the play of the master's words and setting them to work within his own discourse.

Derrida would doubtless deny any suggestion that he has the competence to qualify him as a masterly reader of Joyce's texts, but the irony played out in his argument that there can be no legitimate Joycean competence attests to a refusal on Derrida's part to submit to any existing Joycean body for an evaluation of his competence. Derrida's address to the Ninth International

James Joyce Symposium acknowledges the Joyceans whom he addressed and from whom, "as experts," he feigned to ask for a "diploma in Joyce studies"; but the acknowledgment and request are ironic within the context of Derrida's decision "to interrogate . . . the institution of Joycean experts" (Derrida 1992a:266). For Derrida, there "can be no Joycean competence. . . . no Joycean foundation, no Joycean legitimacy" (Derrida 1992a:282). While denying the possibility of an expertise in Joycean matters, Derrida identifies the name of Elijah as the name that "should be given to all the 'chairs' . . . the 'panels' and 'workshops' organized by" the Joyce Foundation. Playfully establishing his own Joycean legitimacy, he adds, "I too am called Elijah: this name . . . was given me on my seventh day" (Derrida 1992a:284). The student thus indicates his "right" to assume the position of one who can regulate the play of his Joycean masters' words.

Derrida's first extensive talk on Joyce took place in 1982. "Two Words for Joyce" is described by Geoffrey Bennington as "a more or less extemporary talk given at the Centre Georges Pompidou, Paris in November, 1982" (Derrida 1984a:158 n. 1). Geert Lernout states that "Derrida gave [the talk] at the centenary celebrations in Beauborg in November 1982" (Lernout 1990:62). Whichever of these accounts is correct, "Two Words for Joyce" is important in revealing the operations of Joyce's writing within Derrida's speech and the force which Derrida's readings of Joyce have within Derrida's writings.

Derrida's second major talk on Joyce was the "opening address at the Ninth International James Joyce Symposium in Frankfurt." Fritz Senn was responsible for inviting Derrida to speak at the symposium, and many Joyceans who were aware of the "continuing importance" of Joyce in Derrida's work were eager to hear what Derrida had to say. As Derek Attridge points out, however, "few people in the audience could have been prepared for the long, detailed, circuitous, always unpredictable, frequently comic exploration of *Ulysses* that developed out of the apparently innocuous opening, '*Oui, oui, vous m'entendez bien, ce sont des mots français*'" (Attridge 1992b:253).

Derrida read "*Ulysses* Gramophone: Hear Say Yes in Joyce" from a prepared text (which was partially produced with the aid of a cassette recorder, and thus through technology and speech), but in reading the text, his speech echoes Joyce's writing and reveals his desire to evade the linearity and progressive, teleological structures governing many traditional forms of language. Like *Ulysses* itself, "*Ulysses* Gramophone" follows a series of circular patterns. In the same way that Joyce's characters keep crossing each other's paths in cyclical patterns of return, Derrida's essay departs from certain points only to return to them again after circuitous, rhetorical "loops" during which Derrida picks up other themes and motifs in order to let them echo like contrapuntal free voices harmonizing his dominant themes. Attridge sees the essay as a conscious imitation of the double structures of Joyce's texts. It responds to Joyce's writing *and* narrates the details of its own composition: "The essay's wandering path, as it weaves together the story of its own composition, fragments of the text of *Ulysses,* and a number of the issues that Derrida has addressed at length elsewhere, mimes both Joyce's novel (together with its Homeric predecessor) and a crucial aspect of its argument: the necessary connection between chance and necessity" (Attridge 1992b:253).

Although "*Ulysses* Gramophone" focuses on its eponymous text, Derrida's reading of *Ulysses* may well have been filtered through his knowledge of the *Wake.* In the same way that *Finnegans Wake* continually offers fictitious accounts of its creation, Derrida continually returns to the ways in which he created his talk on Joyce. One circle, or "trace" or "relay," moves from the reference to the "Great Battle, Tokio," which Bloom finds in the edition of the *Telegraph* he reads in the Cabman's Shelter, to Derrida's own experience in Tokyo, where he "began to dictate the main ideas [for "*Ulysses* Gramophone"] into a pocket cassette recorder" (Derrida 1992a:259). Derrida keeps returning to his visit to Tokyo, one site of the West's "other," throughout the text. This re-marks Derrida's own alterity (in the East as opposed to the West, where he speaks on Joyce; from the institute of Joyce studies) at the same time that it marks Derrida's shared alterity with the "Tokio" of which Bloom reads in *Ulysses* and with Bloom himself: both experience their shared Judaic heritage as an alterity and both are linked through Japan, the site of the West's "other." Derrida links this site of alterity he shares with Bloom to the creation of his talk, to the theme of postcards (in *Ulysses,* in his text *The Post Card,* and in the bookshop in his Tokyo hotel) as well as to the element of chance.

"[C]ontinuing the chronicle of *my experiences*" in creating his text, Derrida returns to his visit to Tokyo and describes a *chance* encounter with an American tourist. This tourist "leaned over my shoulder and sighed: 'So many books! What is the definitive one? Is there any?' . . . I almost replied, 'Yes, there are two of them, *Ulysses* and *Finnegans Wake*" (Derrida 1992a:265). In identifying *the* definitive book as *two* texts by Joyce, Derrida keeps in play both the singularity he stresses as a hallmark of the event of Joyce's writing and the double structure (of Joyce's texts, of his own countersigning of those texts, and of his own writing as a counterexample to Joyce) by which this singularity doubles and unfolds, as if by chance, in Joyce's two texts.

"Two Words for Joyce"

Like "*Ulysses* Gramophone," "Two Words for Joyce" imitates the cyclical patterns of return informing both *Ulysses* and *Finnegans Wake*. Derrida begins by alluding to the impossibility of reading Joyce, stating "it is always too late with Joyce, I shall say only two words" (Derrida 1984a:145). Derrida's "two words" (which are "*for*" Joyce in all senses of the term) establish the poles of the "double mark" that is so important in both his and Joyce's writings. The immense achievements of Joyce's writing mean "it is always too late with Joyce," and the "two words" Derrida investigates within the context of the impossibility of translation operate as points of departure and return for the cyclical patterns that structure "Two Words for Joyce."

The belatedness of our responses to Joyce is directly linked to Derrida's concern with the translation of "He war" into an anagram of the Hebrew YAHWE. Already anticipating our attempts at translating its languages and identifying its puns, Joyce's narration of the myth of Babel (and the double "babelizing" of the words with which he narrates it) restages the "declared war in language" (Derrida 1984a:146), which defeats our translations by always already having confounded our attempts to translate Joyce into the stable, logical, and traditional unilinear language of the academy. Joyce's dream of a "special institution for his oeuvre" has the effect of turning all of us who are his "readers, writers, critics, teachers" into his dream, "his dream readers, the ones he dreamed of and whom we dream of being in our turn" (Derrida 1992a:74).

The deconstructive concerns emphasized in "Two Words" include the relationships between the reading and writing of written or printed texts and the vocalizing and hearing of those texts within speech. Derrida begins by addressing these relationships before moving on to consider the double bind of translation, which makes translation impossible at the same time that it makes translation the only option for understanding. Derrida moves from the achievements and effects of Joyce's "speechreading" (*FW* 568.31) text to the problems of translation (and the shift from speech to writing and vice versa is itself a particular case of translation) only to return to these achievements and effects in the sort of cyclical pattern that structures "Two Words." During these circuitous articulations of his themes, Derrida also uses the technique he frequently adopts elsewhere in his work of opening up the autobiographical elements in both the general practices of reading and writing and his own specific engagements with particular texts.

The two words on which Derrida focuses his attention are "HE WAR," and the preliminary translation he "sketches" adopts the *Wake*'s own technique of "babelizing": "HE WARS—he wages war . . . he is war, which can also be pronounced by babelizing a bit . . . by Germanizing, then, in Anglo-Saxon, He war: he was—he who was ('I am he who is or who am', says YAHWE). . . . Pushing things a bit, taking the time to draw on the vowel and to lend an ear, it will have been true, *wahr,* that's what can be kept [*garder*] or looked at [*regarder*] in truth" (Derrida 1984a:145). Derrida's concerns with Joyce's babelizing narrative of God, violence, and language return him to the question of historical totality and the history of war that he explored in his reading of Levinas's attempt to separate himself from Husserl's reduction of the "infinite alterity" to the status of the same (Derrida 1978:125).

In the history of the word according to Joyce, languages appear with Yahweh's declaration of war to confound man's language. For Levinas "there is war only *after* the opening of discourse" (Derrida 1978:125; emphasis added). Joyce's reading/rewriting of the historical simultaneity of violence and language support Derrida's argument that the "philosopher (man) must speak and write within this war . . . in which he always already knows himself to be engaged; a war which he knows is inescapable." The word according to Joyce also inscribes the "other" of a correction (and the simultaneous other of correction) to Levinas's view of history as a totality. The history from which "the philosopher cannot escape . . . is the history of the *departures from* totality" (Derrida 1978:117; emphasis added). History is not the totality whose limits Husserl wished to transcend through a univocity that might make it possible to grasp the roots of history at their origins; nor is it the totality Levinas saw "transcended by eschatology, metaphysics or speech. It is transcendence itself," the sort of transcendence at work in the equivocal language with which Joyce articulates systems and orders (of myths, language, war, history, religion, and literature) as other. In the equivocal feigning of Joyce's "Shamwork" language: "Yet is no body present here which was not there before. Only is order othered" (*FW* 613.10, 13–14). This making other of order re-marks the order of the god who declares war in language as the order of the other, and it sets this "other" order to work in confounding the stability of the symbol and triggering the symbol's becoming unmotivated as a sign operating within the infinitude of a play regulated by the order of, precisely, the other.

The section from the *Wake* upon which Derrida fixes his attention explores the complex relationships between the God of the Old Testament, the attempt at building the tower of Babel, the war God declares in destroying the tower, and the ensuing confusion of human languages that makes translation an impossible necessity. One extended passage restages the divine declaration of war on humankind in an imitation of the "rhythm of Biblical writing":

> And let Nek Nekulon extol Mak Makal and let him say unto him: Immi ammi Semmi. And shall not Babel be with Lebab? *And he war.* And he shall open his mouth and answer: I hear, O Ismael, how they laud is only as my loud is one. If Nekulon shall be havonfalled surely Makal haven hevens. Go to, let us extell Makal, yea, let us exceedingly extell. Though you have lien amung your posspots my excellency is over Ismael. Great is him whom is over Ismael and he shall mekanek of Mak Nakulon. And he deed.
>
> Uplouderamainagain!
>
> For the Clearer of the Air from on high has spoken in tumbul-dum tambaldam to his tembledim tombaldoom worrild and, mogu-phono-ised by that phonemanon, the unhappitents of the earth have terrerum-bled from fimament unto fundament and from tweedledeedumms down to twiddledeedees" (*FW* 258.10–24; emphasis added; cited in Derrida 1984a:152–53).

Located close to the center of the printed version of "Two Words," this passage helps provide Derrida's talk with an alternative structure (an "other" structure) to the series of cyclical digressions in which Derrida articulates the mythemes of paternity, (Yahweh's) language, naming, fraternity, warfare, and death. Like the "crease" dividing the two halves of "The Double Session" of *Dissemination,* three spaces or creases divide "Two Words" into four discrete sections. Each of these creases is marked by three asterisks arranged in the shape of an inverted triangle. The middle one of these three creases marked with the inverted triangle of asterisks occurs close to the center of "Two Words." On one side of this crease, Derrida cites an extensive passage from his *Post Card;* on the other side, he cites the passage from the *Wake.*

This produces a frame in which, and from which, the texts of Joyce and Derrida mirror each other, re-creating the double that Derrida marks out in Joyce. The positioning of the passages allows Derrida to explore the numerous ways in which his text, *The Post Card,* is "[a]bove all . . . haunted by Joyce." The two passages mirror each other across the central crease or fold marked by the inverted triangle of three asterisks. The significance of this inverted triangle may be an arbitrary editorial or typesetting choice, but it may also reflect (even as the result of a random choice or selection) Derrida's interest in the Greek letter Delta (Δ) as a perfect letter and a figure for Joyce's ALP. In *Dissemination* he offers an "unacknowledged quotation from Robert Greer Cohn's *L'Oeuvre de Mallarmé: Un coup de Dés*" (Lernout 1990, 60–61): "The triangle with its point downward, the lower part of Solomon's seal, is a traditional symbol of the feminine principle, exploited extensively in *Finnegans Wake*" (Derrida 1981:330).

Exploring the theme of language as a site of warfare, Derrida completes one of his cyclical returns to the passage from the *Wake* and considers Joyce's text as a radical restaging of the mythical events that took place at Babel: "In the landscape immediately surrounding the 'he war', we are, if such a present is possible, and this place, at Babel: at the moment when YAHWEH declares war, HE WAR" (Derrida 1984a, 153–54). Following the example of the *Wake*'s radical anagrams (as ALP's letter, as her words, the *Wake* can be read as "Anna's grammes"), Derrida reads HE WAR as a possible anagram on the name of YAHWEH: "exchange of the final R and the central H in the anagram's throat" (Derrida 1984a:154).

The victim of this war at Babel is Shem the penman, and writers, those who bear his name ("Immi ammi Semmi," "I am Shem"), are punished as "those who, according to Genesis, declare their intention of building the tower in order to make a name for themselves." (Shem the penman uses his pen and penis to build his linguistic and phallic tower even as he participates in what the *Wake* describes as the "wielderfight" of a "penisolate war" [*FW* 3.6].) In Derrida's reading of Joyce's recreation of Babel, God's confounding of the languages of the tower builders is a deconstructive "(con)fusion," and "the Lord . . . deconstructs by speaking the vocable of his choice, the name of confusion, which in the hearing, could be confused with a word indeed signifying 'confusion'" (Derrida 1984a:154).

Love is doubled by its other in the forms necessary to war. Derrida can thus re-mark the destructive act of war "as not necessarily anything other than an election, an act of love." In the *Wake*'s restaging of language-as-warfare, language is also a gesture of love. In support of this hypothesis,

Derrida quotes the passage "for aught I care for the contrary, the all is *where* in love as war and the plane where ... " (*FW* 151.35–152.1; cited in Derrida 1984a:154). This (con)fusion of love and war would be well known to readers of Joyce familiar with Joyce's use of Giordano Bruno's doctrine of the coincidence of contraries, but it is simultaneously a (con)fusion marking Derrida's own ambivalent attitude toward Joyce. On the one hand, Derrida has a deep and abiding respect and admiration for Joyce's work; on the other hand, he can mark the alterity, the "other" of his respect and admiration, which operates within his indebtedness to Joyce. At the conclusion of "Two Words," Derrida completes a cycle that he initiated in his introduction by reciting some of his own words: "'I'm not sure I like Joyce ... I'm not sure he is liked ... except when he laughs ... he's always laughing ... everything is played out in the difference between several tonalities of laughter'" (Derrida 1984a:146, 157).

It is Derrida's understanding of Joyce's writing (an understanding sometimes marked as the alterity of a "not understanding" by the limited historicism and empiricism used against Derrida's reading of Joyce) that marks the finale to "Two Words." This respectful understanding is threefold and expressed in terms of Joyce's completion of the Hegelianlike project that produces, in *Finnegans Wake,* "a little grandson of Western culture in its circular, encyclopedic, Ulyssean and more than Ulyssean totality" (Derrida 1984a:149). It is Derrida's understanding of Joyce's deconstruction of the speech/writing hierarchy in a multilingual text that can be heard in the singularity of one particular language, voice, or accent but read simultaneously in several languages. It is, perhaps above all, an admiring comprehension of Joyce's comedic "revenge with respect to the God of Babel." Reiterating his admiration for Joyce's deconstructive privileging of the female position in language, Derrida concludes "Two Words" with his assessment of the *Wake* as a text that "says 'we' and 'yes' in the end to the Father or to the Lord who speaks loud ... but ... leaves the last word to the woman who in her turn will have said 'we' [Molly's *oui* or yes and ALP's yes to HCE] and 'yes'. Countersigned God, God who countersigneth thyself, God who signeth thyself in us, let us laugh, amen" (Derrida 1984a:158).

"*Ulysses* Gramophone: Hear Say Yes in Joyce"

Derrida's spoken address to Joyceans is a countersignature to Joyce that both affirms and exploits the power of Joyce's writing. In the terms of Derrida's metaphor of Joyce as a "1000th generation computer," it explores the "paradoxical logic" of Derrida's relationship to Joyce as one of "two programmes or two literary 'softwares'" (Derrida 1984a:148). Simultaneously, it offers itself as a positive counterexample to the negation of Derrida's understanding of Joyce by historicist, empirical Joycean critics who attack the reliability of Derrida's work on Joyce. Derrida affirms the power of Joyce's texts by countersigning the double affirmation of *Ulysses,* and within this countersignature he sets to work a "no" to the idea of an exclusive (and excluding), legitimate, academic Joycean expertise. From a certain angle, the entirety of Derrida's countersigning of Joyce's double *yeses* can be read as the attempt to answer the question: "How can you make *no* [the "no" reserved to countersign a statement such as "I am an expert on Joyce who has mastered Joyce's writings"] heard, when you mean it without saying it?" (Derrida 1992a:264). But this "no" operates from within the intricate folds of Derrida's powerful and affirmative, double countersignature to Joyce.

Begun as thoughts spoken into a cassette recorder, mediated through telephone conversations with Jean-Michel Rabaté, then transcribed and modified as language on a page to be spoken before the Ninth International James Joyce Symposium at Frankfurt in 1984, "*Ulysses* Gramophone" operates in what Derrida terms a "telegraphic style" (Derrida 1992a:301). This style invokes and fuses together the composition of Derrida's talk (involving recording, telephoning, speaking, listening, and writing) and the technical metaphors operating in Derrida's response to a writing he describes as a "1000th generation computer" (Derrida 1984a:147). The chain of technological metaphors (Bloom's gramophone, the telephone, the postal system, newspapers, computers) running throughout "*Ulysses* Gramophone" (and at work in the title) are triggered off in the first sentence of the piece following a citation of the double *yeses* concluding Molly's discourse: "*Oui, Oui,* you are *receiving* me, these are French words" (Derrida 1992a: 256; Attridge 1992a:253; emphasis added).

The opening paragraphs of "*Ulysses* Gramophone" function as a rhetorical aporia, a knot tying together the various threads that Derrida unravels during his address. His themes include the impossibility of reading Joyce with any sense of mastery; the technological elements in Joyce's work; the element of chance or randomness produced by a system as complex as that of Joyce's writing; the double binds of translation and citation; and a questioning of the authority and legitimacy with which one might declare oneself an expert on Joyce.

While articulating these themes, Derrida weaves autobiographical narrative together with his reading of Joyce and adopts the rhetorical strategy of addressing his audience directly but as if he were talking to them on a telephone. His rhetoric and narratives are thus played out within the double patterns of Derrida's counterexample to Joyce's double, "doublin'" patterns and between the feigned immediate presence of speech and its distancing through a simulacrum of technology. They sustain and enfold Derrida's interrogation of legitimate, Joycean expertise within the movement from his initial reaffirmation of Joycean affirmation to his own alterity as a rhetorical countersignatory exploring the chance and randomness operating in his readings of Joyce.

The opening of this address affords the opportunity of re-marking how Derrida's themes and strategies are woven together in a double textual play that simultaneously remarks its own other, incorporating a narrative of its own textual composition:

> To be sure [certainty as opposed to the unknown and the element of chance], and I do not need to reinforce my message [self-referential and autobiographical, the transmission of a message] with another phrase, all you need [direct address to the listener and necessity, as opposed to chance] is to have heard the first word, *oui* [a reference to the fact that Derrida is speaking in the French that is an "other" language for many of his auditors and a reiteration of one of the Joycean *yeses* Derrida cited earlier], to know, that is if you understand enough French, that, thanks to the authorization [authority which Derrida will later link to legitimacy in order to interrogate it] graciously bestowed on me by the organizers of this James Joyce Symposium, I shall address you [direct address], more or less, in the language presumed to be mine [the question of one's native tongue and thus the possibility of translation]. (Derrida 1992a:256)

The second paragraph re-marks the taking up of Joyce's writing into the alterity of Derrida's language. Derrida focuses on translation and links Molly's *yeses* with those of his own, thus weaving together his reading of Joyce and his own writing:

> But can *oui* be translated? [translation] This is one of the questions I intend to pose during this talk [self-referential]. . . . The one I began with, just as Molly begins and ends what is too lightly referred to as her monologue [combination of autobiography and Joyce's text along with a hint of the attack that Derrida later makes on Joycean authority], that is, the repetition of a *oui,* is not content just to *mention,* it *uses* in its own way these two *ouis,* the ones that I now quote [translation

and randomness: which *ouis* are being discussed?]. In my opening you could not decide, and you are still incapable of deciding, [self-referentiality, direct address, and the chance that makes decision difficult, if not impossible] if I was saying *oui* to you or if I was quoting. (Derrida 1992a:256)

Much of this negates his audience's ability to make a critical decision. It feigns to restage the moment of madness that re-marks the moment of crisis and decision. Derrida affirms the possibility of that decision, opening up the dual moment of decision and madness we examined in his reading of Foucault. It also prepares for the moment when Derrida will tell members of the Joyce Foundation that there can be no such thing as a Joyce Foundation.

Signing and countersigning both entail taking the same risk of affirmation necessitated in the use of the *yeses* that are the object of the encyclopedic exploration within Derrida's meditation on *Ulysses*. We have seen how Joyce viewed *Ulysses* as separated from madness by a "transparent sheet." Unlike Foucault's writing, which failed to follow and account for the hyperbolic path opened up in the critical moment, Joyce's double countersigning of Homer and Shakespeare opened up the risk of madness, to which Joyce exposed himself in taking affirmative responsibility for the hyperbolic language he assembled into *Ulysses* as a double, positive counterexample to the Hellenic and Hebraic traditions.

The process of quoting or citing is a similar act of affirmation. The citation of a word, phrase, sentence, or passage entails saying yes to that passage in a process of countersigning. In reproducing the words of another, one says yes to those words, and even if one countersigns them with disagreement rather than agreement, one still implicitly says yes: "Now if the act of quoting or mentioning also undoubtedly presupposes some signature, some confirmation of the act of mentioning, this remains implicit and the implicit *oui* is not to be confused with the quoted or mentioned *oui*" (Derrida 1992a:257). In other words, Derrida cites Molly's yes (a yes already signed by Joyce) in French, which involves translation and, in so doing, offers an implicit yes to Molly's yes (and to the yes of Joyce's signature), but this yes is not identical to Molly's. The difference between them involves history and translation, as well as the spaces between fact and fiction and literature and philosophy—the spaces and differences in which Derrida consciously situates himself in order to produce "*Ulysses* Gramophone" as a simultaneously double countersignature to Joyce (positive) and the concept of Joycean expertise (negative).

Derrida begins his first circulation through *Ulysses* with the same metaphor he uses in "Two Words" to describe his readings of *Finnegans Wake*: diving into, or becoming immersed in, Joyce's flowing river of language. In "Two Words" he describes the "endless plunge [that] throws you back onto the river-bank, on the brink of another immersion, *ad infinitum*" (Derrida 1984a:148); in "*Ulysses* Gramophone" he combines the same metaphor with an ironic assertion that he will avoid a circulatory reading of *Ulysses*: "To put an end . . . to circulation or to an interminable circumnavigation, to avoid the aporia [with which "*Ulysses* Gramophone" begins] with a view to a better beginning, I threw myself in the water . . . and I decided to open myself, together with you, to a chance encounter" (Derrida 1992a:258).

This notion of a "chance encounter" and the play of randomness in his reading of *Ulysses* is a rhetorical strategy that simultaneously re-marks the risks operating in the play of writing. The position of the "I" in language can offer no more than a simulacrum of stability and control. The alterity of language and the "other" of the "I" are always at work in a way that can undermine the seemingly confident control of language by, and from, the position of the "I." Derrida allows the elements of randomness and chance to contaminate the readings of *Ulysses* with which he prepared his address to the symposium; but as that address was prepared in advance, the "chance encounter" could only *appear* as chance to the audience. This enables Derrida to use chance and randomness as a way of bringing his audience to an experience of his, and their own, indecision. They cannot decide if Derrida's reading preprogrammed a feigned chance encounter or does in fact trace a play that chance produced as he prepared his address. At the same time, randomness and chance are always necessarily a part of any reading, and it is this aspect of his reading of *Ulysses* that Derrida emphasizes during his "aimless wanderings" through the text of "*Ulysses* Gramophone."

Reading *Ulysses* like "an immense postcard" (Derrida 1992a:260), Derrida begins with "the coincidence of meeting" passage in "Eumaeus" (*U* 567). (As Derek Attridge notes, Derrida refers to the 1968 Penguin edition of *Ulysses* [Attridge 1992b:256] but uses the French 1948 Gallimard edition in his calculation of the number of *ouis* in the text [Derrida 1992a:306 n. 25].) Moving on via references to the "*Lacus Mortis*" (*U* 411), Derrida opens up the complex network of a "trace" or "relay" of postcards in *Ulysses*. Noting that J.J. shares Joyce's initials— "not just any initials" (Derrida 1992a:260)—Derrida translates J.J.'s "opinion" that "a postcard is a publication" in which "an action might lie" (*U* 320), as "there would be cause for a certain action to be pursued before the law, to sue, but also that the action itself might tell an untruth" (Derrida 1992a:260).

The relay of postcards linking Bloom, Molly, Gerty, Flynn, Reggy Wylie, and Breen constitutes a "discursive" or "narrative path" that Derrida uses to return to an "ineluctable problem of method" that he previously explored in *The Post Card:* in the operations of human desire in social groups, in language and communication, and in "genealogical fantasies, with their generic cross-overs and chance disseminations, a dream of legitimation. . . . we can never tell who belongs to whom, what to whom, what to what, who to what. There is no subject of belonging, no more than there is an owner of the postcard: it remains without any assigned addressee" (Derrida 1992a: 261).

From this relay of postcards, Derrida opens up two more relays that move in opposite but related directions, eventually making contact with each other again as they are double parts of the same singular textual economy. These relays follow two paths similar to those we saw Derrida map out in his reading of Foucault. The first can be read as the hyperbolic path that can admit unexpected encounters and allow for the operations that chance or random encounters produce. The other is the path of reason that treats the chance encounter as "other" to produce a rational explanation for it. Of course these two paths are both a part of the same economy: the "relationship between reason, madness, and death is an economy, a structure of deferral whose irreducible originality must be respected" (Derrida 1978:62).

Following one relay, Derrida moves from Bloom's telephone conversations and the gramophone he imagines as a device for listening to the voices of the dead to the figure of Elijah, the unexpected guest whose appearance is determined by a logic identifying Elijah as the "other" for those who are his host and who treat his arrival as chance and unexpected, even though they must be prepared for the "chance" of his arrival. Derrida then uses the figure of the prophetic "circumciser," Elijah, as a metaphor for Joyce's readers ("No, Elijah is you: you are the Elijah of *Ulysses,* who is presented as a large telephone exchange . . . the marshalling yard, the network through which all information must transit" [Derrida 1992a:285–86]); as a "synec-doche of Ulyssean narration, at once smaller and greater than the whole" (Derrida 1992a:286); and as a figure of the apocalyptic "operator of the telephone exchange" (Derrida 1992a:289) who could connect all the possible narrative and signifying lines of communication criss-crossing *Ulysses* as well as the innumerable lines of exchange between the text and its readers.

Identifying the Joyceans he addresses with the prophet reinforces Derrida's position as one Susan Handelman calls "heretical hermeneutic." Using this hermeneutic to explore his own readings of Joyce, Derrida allows the figures he generates from Elijah to proliferate, identifying himself with the prophet: "And even if it were true, and even if, yes, it is true, you would not believe me if I told you that I too am called Elijah: this name is not inscribed, no, on my official documents, but it was given me on my seventh day" (Derrida 1992a:284). He then moves on to explain that the "chair on which the new-born baby boy is held [as part of a ritual within the Hebrew religion] is called 'Elijah's chair'" (Derrida 1992a:285). Because the Joyceans whom he addresses are "Elijah," Derrida can count himself among their number; because he bears Elijah's name, he is even more Joycean than they; because the name does not appear on his "official documents," he, like they, lacks legitimate support for a claim to Joycean expertise.

Derrida links the hyperbolic relay generated from the postcard, through the telephone, to the figure of Elijah back into another ironic rhetorical strategy structuring "*Ulysses* Gramophone." This strategy provides the ground for his questioning of the authority of the James Joyce Foundation.

This second relay generated from Derrida's meditation on the postcards in *Ulysses* and his reading of the text as "an immense postcard" follows the same shift from postcards through telephone communications and gramophones to the figure of Elijah. It offers itself as more rational, accounting for random events as chance encounters subsumable by the logic of factual, autobiographical history. Intersecting at certain points with the first relay, this second one detours through Derrida's personal experiences of buying postcards in Tokyo and preparing the address for the symposium: "So I am in the process of buying postcards in Tokyo, pictures of lakes, and apprehensive about the intimidating talk to be given before the 'Joyce scholars' on the subject of *yes* in *Ulysses,* and on the institution of Joyce Studies" (Derrida 1992a:264).

Moving along this logical, autobiographical relay from postcards to the telephone, Derrida records a telephone conversation with his friend Jean-Michel Rabaté: "When Jean-Michel Rabaté phoned me, I had, then, already decided to interrogate, if we can put it like that, the *yeses* of *Ulysses* as well as the institution of Joycean experts, and also to question what happens when the word *yes* is written, quoted, repeated, archived, recorded, gramophoned, or is the subject of translation or transfer" (Derrida 1992a:266).

This second relay draws together the *yeses* in *Ulysses* and the title of Derrida's address through the technical, logical metaphors (as opposed to the hyperbolic metaphors generated from Elijah) of telegraphy, transmission, and "gramophoning": "a title crossed my mind with a kind of irresistible brevity, the authority of a telegraphic order: *hear say yes in Joyce*. . . . So, you are receiving me, Joyce's saying *yes* but also the saying of the *yes* that is heard." Exploiting the French pun on "hearsay [*ouï-dire*]" and "'hear say yes,' *l'oui-dire*," Derrida turns to the relationship between speech and writing that is so important in his deconstructive projects. Explaining that this "untranslatable homonymy [*ouï-dire* and *l'oui-dire*] can be heard . . . rather than read *with the eyes*—the last word, *eyes* . . . giving itself to a reading of the grapheme *yes* rather than a hearing of it," Derrida concludes: "*Yes* in *Ulysses* can only be a mark at once written and spoken, vocalized as a grapheme and written as a phoneme, *yes, in a word, gramophoned*" (Derrida 1992a:267).

Like "Two Words," "*Ulysses* Gramophone" is organized by a series of circular relays operating around the doubling divide of a fold or crease. The two intersecting relays (the reading of *Ulysses* as a postcard and the autobiographical preparation of the address, Derrida's spoken postcard to his audience) both link up with the double structure with which Derrida "interrogates" Joyce scholars and the "institution of Joyce Studies." The first part of this double structure takes the form of a confession in which Derrida admits his fears, his intimidation, and his apprehension at speaking on Joyce to an audience of experts on Joyce's work; the second part consists of a denial of the possibility of any kind of Joycean authority or expertise that reveals the irony of the initial confession. One of the folds or creases within this double structure is provided by the figure of Elijah who also acts as a link between the two relays we have examined.

Confessing his intimidation at speaking in front of Joyce scholars, Derrida declares, "I am too intimidated. Nothing intimidates me more than a community of experts in Joycean matters." He then acknowledges the honor of being asked to address these "experts": "When I agreed to speak before you, before the most intimidating assembly in the world, before the greatest concentration of knowledge on such a polymathic work, I was primarily aware of the honour that was being paid me." Before this acknowledgment, however, Derrida has already declared his intention in questioning the concepts of legitimacy and competence that he seems to accept in referring to his audience as experts: "I had decided . . . to put before you the question of competence, of legitimacy, and of the Joycean institution. Who has a recognized right to speak of Joyce, to write on Joyce, and who does this well? What do competence and performance here consist of?" (Derrida 1992a:279).

The first explicit shift from the humble tone of this apologia could be

Derrida's expression of the suspicion he felt when he accepted the invitation to speak before the symposium: "If I have accepted, it is mainly because I suspected some perverse challenge in a legitimation so generously offered." This is followed by a Socratic, ironic admission of incompetence aimed, one suspects, at Joyceans who might dismiss Derrida's work. Shifting from the second person (with which he addresses the audience for much of the address) to the more neutral third person, Derrida declares that "Incompetence, as *they* (the 'other', absent Joyce experts [emphasis added]) are aware, is the profound truth of my relationship to this work which I know after all *only directly* [my emphasis], through hearsay [Derrida's *oui-dire* and the subtitle of his address], through rumours [Derrida elsewhere reveals his knowledge of the importance of "rumours" in Joyce's writings], through what people say, second-hand exegeses, readings that are always partial [for Derrida *all* readings of Joyce are partial]" (Derrida 1992a:280).

Employing a Ulysseanlike cunning, Derrida declares his intention of revealing a "deception" that is simultaneously his own deception in using "incompetence" to describe "the profound truth of [his] relationship to Joyce" *and* the deception of those "experts" who claim that Derrida is incompetent: "For these experts, I said to myself, the time has come for the deception to [be] made evident, and how could it be demonstrated or denounced better than at the opening of a large symposium?" After a lengthy disquisition on the concepts of competence, legitimacy, and expertise in Joyce studies, Derrida sets aside his irony: "Basically, there can be no Joycean competence, in the certain and strict sense of the concept of competence, with the criteria of evaluation and legitimation that are attached to it. There can be no Joycean foundation, no Joycean family; there can be no Joycean legitimacy" (Derrida 1992a:282).

At the same time that he declares this impossibility of competence, Derrida also claims a certain competence for himself. We have seen how he identifies himself with Elijah ("I too am called Elijah"). Immediately after this, he declares that Elijah's "name [and thus his own, "other" name] should be given to all the 'chairs' of Joycean studies, to the 'panels' and 'workshops' organized by your foundation" (Derrida 1992a:285). In other words, Derrida's "other" name of Elijah should be the name of the study of Joyce at all the symposiums. Those Joyceans whom Derrida also identifies as Elijah ("you are the Elijah of *Ulysses*") would also give their names to the chairs of the symposiums, but Derrida identifies himself as the outsider who is both the "guest" of the symposium and the Elijah whose "second coming" and "passing through" Joyceans "are awaiting" (Derrida 1992a:284).

Throughout this playful combination of his reading of *Ulysses*, the narrative of his autobiography, and his interrogation of Joyce studies, Derrida expresses the same tone of comic celebration and admiration for Joyce that concludes "Two Words." He again considers Joyce in relationship to Hegel, who is listed (albeit in the ironic phrase "without mentioning Hegel") with other major Western writers as being incapable of calculating the scope and achievements of Joyce's "feat" of an "archivization and consultation of data unheard of . . . for all the grandfathers [Plato, Shakespeare, Dante, Vico, and Hegel] whom I have just named, omitting Homer" (Derrida 1992a:280).

Invoking Hegel's philosophical, encyclopedic project, Derrida allows that the "Joyce scholar has the right to dispose of the totality of competence in the encyclopedic field of the *universitas.*" In having at hand Joyce's "computer of all memory," the scholar "plays with the entire archive of culture — at least of what is called Western culture, and, in it, of that which returns to itself according to the Ulyssean circle of the encyclopedia" (Derrida 1992a:281).

The conclusion of "*Ulysses* Gramophone" reiterates the quotation of Molly's *yeses* and emphasizes the comedic, laughter-producing, and communally shared lifting of repression of *Ulysses* that Derrida stresses in much of the address: "Yes, yes, this is what arouses laughter, and we never laugh alone, as Freud rightly said, never without sharing something of the same repression. Or, rather, this is what leads to laughter, just as it, and the id, lead to thought. And just as it, and the id, give quite simply, beyond laughter and beyond the *yes,* beyond the *yes/no/yes* of the *me/not-me, ego/not-ego* which can always turn towards the dialectic" (Derrida 1992a:308).

CHAPTER 7

Speaking of Joyce (II)

Joyce, Deconstruction, and Feminism

THE THIRD TIME DERRIDA SPOKE extensively on Joyce was during an interview with Derek Attridge "in Laguna Beach over two days in April 1989" (Attridge 1992a:33). As the title implies, "'This Strange Institution Called Literature': An Interview with Jacques Derrida" is more concerned with Derrida's ideas on literature than his specific ideas on Joyce; but Derrida cites Joyce's work to express some of his specific concerns about literature's alterity. Pointing toward a possible "logic" for the singularity of a text, Derrida outlines his response to Joyce as the response of an "other" in the "particular, quite single moment" of his own attempts to account for, and countersign, Joyce's writing (Derrida 1992a:70).

The singularity of Joyce's writing is doubled by Derrida's response to it. Linking these double singularities with the repetition necessary to language's iterability, Derrida reiterates *Ulysses*' double yeses as the countersignature of his own reading and writing in response to Joyce's text (and that external text is the "other" of Derrida's), explaining how this countersigning entails a double responsibility for that text: "[t]his countersigning response . . . which is responsible (for itself and for the other), says 'yes' to the work, and again 'yes, this work was there before me, without me, I testify', even if it begins by calling for the co-respondent countersignature" (Derrida 1992a:70; emphasis added).

In addition to providing Derrida with exemplars for some of the specific structural and textual operations he uses in deconstructing writing and allowing literature to contaminate philosophy, Joyce's texts also provide Derrida with a series of important touchstones on which he tests his ideas about literary and philosophical writing and the nature of the relationships between the two.

Derrida's general views on these topics specify how Joyce's writing has contributed to the development of deconstructive theory. Covering a diverse range of topics including the nature of philosophy and literature, the relationships between the two, the purposes of his own writing, and the much overlooked historical basis for deconstruction, Derrida's discussion cites Joyce on a number of occasions as a measure for evaluating his concerns about both literature and philosophy.

Derrida consciously positions his writing on the borders between philosophy and literature, marking this positioning as autobiographical. Discussing his "autobiographical" and "adolescent desire" to write, he explains that this desire "was as obscure as it was compulsive, both powerless and authoritarian." It "directed [him] toward something in writing which was neither" literature nor philosophy (Derrida 1992b:34). Derrida keeps writing because of a "totalization or gathering up," and it is clear from many of his statements about Joyce that we have already examined that Joyce's singularity consists in part of just such a totalizing and gathering. Joyce is clearly a part of Derrida's "internal polylogue," and Derrida was initially led to read and explore Joyce's writing by an "adolescent dream of keeping a trace of all the voices which were traversing [him]" (Derrida 1992b:34–35).

Joyce's figure in Derrida's "internal polylogue" plays a major role in Derrida's specific writing strategies by providing a model of the literary and philosophical consolidation of history, which Derrida sees as a simultaneous culmination of the empirical past and a prescriptive model of writing for the future of a "new order." While *Ulysses* "arrives like one novel among others that you place on your bookshelf and inscribe in a genealogy," and, like other works of literature, "has its ancestry and its descendants," it is unique for Derrida in having enabled Joyce to achieve his dream of a "special institution for his oeuvre, inaugurated by it like a new order." Derrida sees himself as having "to understand and share [Joyce's] dream" by making it his own, "recognizing [his own dream] in it" and "shar[ing] it in *belonging to the dream* of Joyce, in *taking a part in it* . . . walking around in *his* space." Joyce has a universal impact on the literary institution and a constitutional effect on his readers: "Aren't we, today," Derrida asks, "people or characters in part constituted (as readers, writers, critics, teachers) *in* and *through* Joyce's dream? Aren't we Joyce's dream, his dream readers, the ones he dreamed of and whom we dream of being in our turn?" (Derrida 1992b:74).

A feature of Joyce's writing that most concerns Derrida is its production of the double spaces we have already explored and will explore in more detail in the next chapters. These spaces, which Derrida reinscribes in the double, textual, and autobiographical spaces of his own writing, are "not only [those] of an instituted *fiction* but also [of] a *fictive institution* which in principle allows one to say everything." Joyce's "saying everything" is a specific and precise example of the Hegelianlike encyclopedic project "to gather, by translating, all figures into one another, to totalize by formalizing." This "saying everything" "is also [the movement] to break out of . . . prohibitions. To *affranchise oneself* . . . in every field where law can lay down law." For Derrida, literature possesses a potentially liberating power that "in principle," "tends . . . to defy or lift the law" (Derrida 1992b:36).

In "*Ulysses* Gramophone" Joyce's signature and the *yes* occupying, and occupied by, Joyce's readers have the "destination" of "destroying the very root of [the] competence" that they make possible. They are also capable of "deconstructing the university institution, its internal or interdepartmental divisions, as well as its contract with the extra-university world" (Derrida 1992a:283). What Derrida says of the institution of literature in general is therefore clearly applicable to the Joyce institution: "it is an institution which tends to overflow the institution" (Derrida 1992b:36).

"This Strange Institution Called Literature" reveals Derrida's reservations about, and mistrust of, certain popular views of deconstruction, and these are relevant to his reading of Joyce as a writer without whom deconstruction would not have been possible. These reservations include the view we have already seen of Derrida as "very much a historian, very historicist." Derrida does not trust those "people [who] believe or have an interest in making believe" that deconstruction is not concerned with history (Derrida

1992b:54). As we have noted several times, Derrida clearly views Joyce's writing as performing a historical task in its gathering together and encyclopedic totalizing of Western culture, even if it does so by fictionalizing it within the "fictive" institution of literature. The reason Derrida used Joyce as a counterexample to the views of Husserl and Levinas is that his texts offer a model of history attempting to free itself from the empirical and historicist ideas of history that we saw deconstructed by Derrida's readings of those philosophers.

There is a "sort of paradoxical historicity in the experience of writing" that may help explain why some people view Derrida's work as unhistorical or even antihistorical. The paradox is produced by the opposition between history as a series of empirical, objective past events, which it is the historian's duty to record, and the vital, fictive re-creation of those events within the presence of a narrative that sets them to work in the re-creation of a necessary but unmotivated account of history as the source for fictive narratives. A "writer can be ignorant or naive in relation to the historical tradition which bears him or her, or which s/he transforms, invents [or] displaces" (Derrida 1992b:54), but the same writer's experience may be a vital historical experience: "I wonder whether, even in the absence of historical awareness or knowledge s/he doesn't 'treat' history in the course of an experience which is more significant, more alive, more *necessary*...than that of some professional 'historians' naively concerned to 'objectify' the content of a science."

This "alive" and "necessary" treatment of history is by no means limited to a writer such as Joyce, although Derrida obviously sees Joyce's treatment of history in this light: "What I have just suggested is as valid for Joyce, that immense allegory of historical memory, as for Faulkner, who doesn't write in such a way that he gathers together at every sentence, and in several languages at once, the whole of Western culture" (Derrida 1992b:55).

What reassures Derrida that he likes Joyce is the laughter and *jouissance* Joyce's writings release in his readers. Laughter is a means of awaking from the nightmare of history by loosening the repressive, historical, and empirical, linear suppression of the play of language's inherent polysemy. The lifting of repression marked by Joyce's laughter is an important deconstructive effect of Joyce's writing and deconstruction in general: "Effective deconstruction. Deconstruction perhaps has the effect, if not the mission, of liberating forbidden *jouissance*" (Derrida 1992b:56).

Derrida's mistrust of those who view deconstruction as unhistorical is linked to their lack of humor and their role as what Derrida terms "masters of 'kettle logic'," who are the "all-out adversaries of 'deconstruction'." It isn't difficult to imagine that a number of these adversaries would also dislike Joyce for the laughter he provokes, because they "blame those they call the 'deconstructionists' for depriving them of their habitual delectation in the reading of great works or the rich treasures of tradition, and simultaneously for being too playful, for taking too much pleasure, for saying what they like for their own pleasure, etc."

From Derrida's perspective, readers of Joyce who appreciate the gift of laughter that his writings offer appreciate deconstruction even if they choose to avoid using the term. On the other hand, those who use the "ridiculous vocabulary" of "deconstructionism" and "deconstructionists" (terms which recently have been further comically transformed into "deconstructionalism" and "deconstructionalists") "understand in some obscure way that the 'deconstructionists' . . . are not those who most deprive themselves of pleasure" (Derrida 1992b:56).

The laughter and playfulness Derrida admires in Joyce's writing lack neither seriousness nor logic. Both are at work in Joyce's writing even as it overturns the hierarchy privileging seriousness and logic over playfulness and the logic(s) of the other ("other" logics such as those of the unconscious, of anagrams and paronomasia). The *Wake*'s serious-minded professor, who accidentally punctures a manuscript with his fork while eating his breakfast and then devotes his time to establishing the significance of the holes in the manuscript, not only offers a satiric view of academics and their projects but also brings low a sterile self-important sense of seriousness, doing so within a network of play.

Ulysses and *Finnegans Wake* are the texts Derrida most admires for their deconstructive effects (including the jouissance and repression-lifting laughter they provoke and unleash). We have already looked at why Derrida respects the uniqueness and historical singularity of both texts, recognizing that each "work takes place just once" and that its uniqueness is "historical through and through" (Derrida 1992b:67). At the same time, there is a paradox to the singularity of Joyce's writing that is at work in the singularity of all the literary texts Derrida admires. The singularity of the "date and the signature. . . . which constitute or institute the very body of the work, on the edge *between* the 'inside' and the 'outside', of the work, . . . necessitates an attention to history, context and genre" (Derrida 1992b:67–68). Joyce's "condensation of history, of language, of the encyclopedia, remains here indissociable from an *absolutely* singular signature, and therefore also of a date, of a language, of an autobiographical inscription" (Derrida 1992b:43).

At the same time, the "absolute singularity" of Joyce's texts (and of those by writers like Ponge, Bataille, Artaud) is "never given as a fact, an object or existing thing . . . in itself, it is announced in a paradoxical experience." The paradox is that an "absolute, absolutely pure singularity, if there were one, would not even show up, or at least would not be available for reading. To become readable, it has to be *divided,* to *participate* and *belong*" (Derrida 1992b:68). This same paradox is at work in the equivocity of Joyce's writing we considered while looking at Derrida's comparison of Joyce and Husserl. Joyce's encyclopedic project of absorbing and archiving as many fragments as he could from Western culture, from its classical and religious institutions, its languages, epistemes, mythemes, and narratives, required some form of univocity that would make these fragments reiterable in a communicable form.

For Derrida, Joyce successfully subsumes innumerable metaphysical concepts such as platonic ideal forms, the Christian, paternal creator, the unity of the subject (of the self, of divine beings, and so on) and the clear distinctions between a superior good and inferior evil (as well as the chains of other signifiers attached to these two). Paradoxically (and this paradox is related to that of Joyce's "singularity"), his writing is "laden with obvious and canonical 'metaphysical' theses," but "the operation of [this] writing" has "more powerful 'deconstructive' effects than a text proclaiming itself radically revolutionary without in any way affecting the norms or modes of traditional writing" (Derrida 1992b:50).

We have seen a simple example of this paradox as it is found in the *Wake*'s repetition of the metaphysical proclamation "I am Alpha and Omega . . . saith the Lord, which is, and which was, and which is to come" (Rev. 1.8) in "Anna was, Livia is, Plurabelle's to be" (*FW* 215.24). The words of the Bible's male god and creator are deconstructively overturned as they are assigned to Joyce's maternal word and wife. The traditional, historical privileging of the male over the female is continually overturned in Joyce's writing as the dissonant voices of the males (Bloom, Boylan, Stephen, HCE, Shem, and Shaun) emerge from within a language identified as female (Molly's soliloquy, Issy's "gramma's grammar," ALP's "languo of flows," Anna's grammes).

When the *Wake* is read as the dream of the male HCE and a narrative of his phallic "phall" (*FW* 4.15) and subsequent resurrection (and re-erection), celebrating the retumescence of his "Hot and hairy, hugon ["huge one"] . . . where the falskin begins. Smoos as an infams" (*FW* 621.24–25), it obviously operates in a phallocentric mode. In "thinking of Joyce," however, Derrida identifies Joyce's work as one of those "which are highly

'phallocentric' in their semantics, their intended meaning, even their theses"
but "produce paradoxical effects, paradoxically antiphallocentric through
the audacity of a writing which in fact disturbs the order or the logic of
phallocentrism or touches on limits where things are reversed" (Derrida
1992b:50).

The paradoxes created in the deconstructive effects of Joyce's writing
may help answer the question of if his writing can be read as feminist. The
arguments for and against Joyce-as-feminist are too numerous and complex
to restate here, as is the evidence (historical, political, contextual, biographical, textual) used to support them. There is little doubt many femi-
nists would see Joyce's personal views on the difficulties of living with
women, on their "amorality," their supposed lack of philosophical skills, as
well as his antifeminist statements (Ellmann 1983:435, 529, 168, 634) as
conclusive proof that Joyce was antifeminist or misogynistic. The important
question from Derrida's perspective, however, is how Joyce's *writings* produce a criticism of phallocentrism and deconstruct their own phallocentric
effects.

Noting that much academic, feminist criticism is "an identifiable institu-
tional phenomenon contemporary with the appearance of what is called
deconstruction in the modern sense," Derrida points out that this con-
temporaneity does not mean feminist criticism "necessarily or always . . .
depend[s] on it." Feminism does, however, "belong to the same configuration and participate in the same movement, the same motivation," even
though the "strategies can . . . be different, be opposed here and there, and
inequalities can appear" (Derrida 1992b:57–58). The most obvious shared
movement between feminist criticism and deconstruction is that toward a
critique of phallocentrism.

For Derrida, "there is no text before and outside reading," and in the
Derrida after and inside Joyce's text we have examined so far, he pays considerable attention to the positions of the female. Much of "*Ulysses* Gramophone" draws on Molly's discourse to stress the valuable lifting of repression provoked by her affirmative, laughter-releasing yeses. The yeses are
signed by Molly and countersigned by Joyce. For Derrida, the "yes would
then be that of woman—and not just that of the mother, the flesh, the earth,
as is . . . said of Molly's *yeses* in the majority of readings devoted to her:
'Penelope, bed, flesh, earth, monologue' [Derrida cites Gilbert 1963:328]
. . . and here Joyce is no more competent than anyone else" (Derrida
1992a:287). Setting aside this question of competence, Derrida values
Joyce's creation of Molly's female yes for expressing "the truth of a certain

truth," but he sees the "law of gender" as "overdetermined and infinitely more complicated, whether we are dealing with sexual or grammatical gender, or again with rhetorical technique." To call Molly's soliloquy a monologue (in the sense of one word, one set of words or even one logic) is, for Derrida, "to display a somnambulistic carelessness" (Derrida 1992a:288).

Deconstruction reveals the inadequacy of traditional, phallocentric, literary taxonomy in dealing with the complex, double paradoxical jouissance of literary discourse. Molly's soliloquy is much more complex than the generic term monologue (and all that term implies) can reveal. It is not regulated by a singular or monologic, and its effects extend well outside the limits of its borders. In its recuperation of events in Molly's life that take place before June 16, the signifying play of Molly's night thoughts extends beyond the limits of *Ulysses*' narration of that day (this, of course, is also true of many other sections of the text). The shifting perspectives on the myriad subjects (including Bloom, home, strangeness, music, trains, men, women, menstruation, ejaculation, clothing, Howth, Gibraltar, oysters, Stephen, Italian) of Molly's discourse produce many more effects than those of the sort of singular thematic development so often associated with monologues.

Derrida describes his attempts at counting all the yeses occurring in *Ulysses* and records that he found "more than 222 in all, of which more than a quarter, at least 79, are in Molly's so-called monologue" (Derrida 1992a:306). From one perspective, he reads *Ulysses* as a vast, complex network of affirmation sustained and regulated by these yeses and their effects. He asks is it possible to read the yeses circulating through Molly's soliloquy "without making them resonate with all the *yeses* that prepare the way for them, correspond to them, and keep them hanging on at the other end of the line throughout the whole book?" (Derrida 1992a:288).

His answer is that such a reading is not possible. Even though Molly "is not Joyce . . . her *yes* circumnavigates and circumcises, encircling the last chapter of *Ulysses,* since it is at once her first and her last word, her send-off . . . and her closing fall: 'Yes because he never did' and finally 'and yes I said yes I will Yes'" (Derrida 1992a:288). Molly's final yes operates as a signature to the text in its typographical placement (the "eschatological final 'Yes' occupies the place of the signature at the bottom right of the text" [Derrida 1992a:288]) and as a countersignature to the signature of the text itself and Joyce's signature: "Even if one distinguishes, as one must, Molly's 'yes' from that of *Ulysses,* of which she is but a figure and a moment, even if one distinguishes . . . these two signatures . . . from that of Joyce, they read each other and call out to each other. To be precise, they call to each other across a *yes*, which always inaugurates a scene of call and request: it confirms and countersigns." The affirmation of *Ulysses*, like all affirmation, "demands *a prior* confirmation, repetition, safekeeping, and the memory of the *yes*" (Derrida 1992a:288).

Derrida's reading of Joyce's yeses supports a feminist critique of phallogocentrism by identifying the limits of its criticism. Derrida's attempt at counting all the yeses in *Ulysses* can be read as a humorous parody of a linear, empirical, and historicist attempt at providing objective statistical proof for the thesis that each yes operates only within the immediate context in which it appears. In effect, such cataloging and "proving" must say "no" to the possibility that each yes calls, confirms, and countersigns its counterparts across the borders of the contexts in which each yes is situated. The phallogocentric goal of dismantling puns in order to identify their component parts and explain why they may produce laughter is a serious task worthy of the *Wake*'s "grave Brofèsor," but it cannot account for, or explain, the laughter or jouissance that can come from reading the pun. It must first forget and then deny that the primary purpose of the pun is to provoke laughter in an affirmation of language's communicative vitality. Derrida's attempt to affirm the power of Joyce's yeses demands a practice of writing to countersign, affirm, and remember the laughter that in "the buginning" was the Joycean "woid" (*FW* 378.29). Such a writing practice entails loosening the control of language's polysemy by the model of the line and a willingness to risk negation and denial for the possibility of positive affirmation. It is a writing practice seeking to remove the bar sustaining the logical distinction of the either/or in favor of affirmatively conjoining either/or with and.

In exploring the relay of yeses in *Ulysses*, Derrida opens up the double space of writing made possible and sustained by this relay. There is Molly's female yes countersigning Joyce's yes, and both are at work in the affirmative yes of the text itself. While a phallogocentric, contextualizing taxonomy might try to attach gender to the yeses of Joyce and Molly, Derrida suggests that the yes operates beyond gender: "Before asking who signs, if Joyce is or is not Molly . . . ; before chattering about sexual difference as duality and expressing one's convictions as to . . . Molly as 'onesidedly womanly woman' . . . Molly, the beautiful plant, the herb or *pharmakon*— or the 'onesidedly masculine' character of James Joyce . . . one will ask oneself what a signature is" (Derrida 1992a:295–96). The answer to this question is involved with the "What is?" that is the founding question of philosophy. The signature "requires a *yes* more 'ancient' than the question

'what is?' since this question presupposes it, a *yes* more ancient than knowledge [and knowledge even of being and gender]." "One will ask oneself for
what reason the *yes* always appears as a [doubled] *yes, yes*. I say the *yes* and
not the word 'yes,' because there can be a *yes* without a word" (Derrida
1992a:296).

Like Molly's affirmative yeses, the language of *Finnegans Wake* supports
a view of Joyce's writing as sharing the feminist critique of phallocentrism.
We have already seen that its circular narratives tell the tale of HCE's phallic
"phall" and celebrate his equally phallic resurrection, but this is only one of
the *Wake*'s multiple narratives; and all of these narratives are articulated in
a language that identifies itself as ALP's "languo of flows" (*FW* 621.22), a
female language operating at the margins of the "limpidy marge" on which
ALP has "made me hoom" (*FW* 624.14). There are numerous narratives
marked or signed by figures of masculine gender, but these are enfolded in
a metalanguage identified with the metaphoric female cycle of water (and
blood) in which the Liffey flows out to sea only to return through the natural cycle of evaporation, condensation, and precipitation that feeds the
small brook of the Liffey as it flows from mountains south of Dublin. We
have seen Anna Livia Plurabelle's name confirm the female nature of the
text's metalanguage in tracing the evolution of Western languages from the
Classical Greek, *Ana,* through, or "via," the Latin, *Livia,* to the modern
French, *plu, belle,* and *elle.*

The babble of ALP's brook puns with the *Wake*'s use of the story of Babel,
and the last Joycean passage Derrida considers in his "Two Words for
Joyce," ends with two words (an "other" "two words" for Joyce) that are
a double inscription of the same in the familiar, maternal name "Mummum" (Anna's name is also a homonym of the Turkish word for mother
[McHugh 1980:104]). This double inscription of singularity (*mum* is singular; the infantlike repetition doubles its singularity) concludes a passage in
which the phallogocentric subject of the paternal creator is converted in the
traversal through laughter into this double signifier of maternity and silence: "Loud, heap miseries upon us yet entwine our arts with laughters
low! Ha he hi ho hu. Mummum" (*FW* 259.7–10).

Derrida reads the "Ha he hi ho hu" sequence as the final, expiring articulations of the "Loud," or Lord, the "He" who declares "war," and confounds the languages of those attempting to build the tower of Babel. This
"last vocalization, the series of expiring vowels, voices out of breath,"
marks the final cadence of the "Loud," who "resounds . . . gives himself to
be heard . . . articulates himself and makes himself heard right up to the end"
(Derrida 1984a:157).

In his reading of this passage, Derrida affirms the maternal voice marking and countersigning the expiring, final articulations of the "He" who is at "war," and this maternal voice can be read as an echo of Molly's ultimate "Yes": "The final 'Mummum,' maternal syllable right near the end, could, if one so wished, be made to resound with the feminine 'yes' in the last line of *Ulysses,* the yes of Mrs Bloom, of ALP, or of any 'wee' girl, as has been noted, Eve, Mary, Isis, etc. The Great Mother on the side of the creation and the fall" (Derrida 1984a:157).

Derrida follows William York Tindall's tracing of the female relay in which "the word 'hill' plays more or less innocently with the French personal pronoun 'il', to say nothing of the 'île': 'As he [HCE] is the hill in Joyce's familial geography, so she is the river [. . .]. This 'wee' (or *oui*) girl is Eve, Mary, Isis, any woman you can think of, and a *poule*—at once a riverpool, a whore, and a little hen'" (Tindall 1969:4; Derrida 1984a:157).

From the "Mummum" concluding this section Derrida draws our attention to the beginning of the lessons section following it: "And if the page is turned, after a broad blank, there is the beginning of Book II, Chapter 2 (I content myself here with letting read and resound)" (Derrida 1984a:157):

> As we there are where are we are we there   UNDE ET UBI.
> from tomtittot to teetootomtotalitarian. Tea
> tea too oo. (*FW* 260.1–3 and right-hand margin)

Derrida does not pursue a reading of this section, but he has already taught his listeners how to. Using some of the deconstructive "non-concepts" Derrida uncovers at work in Joyce's writing, we can read these opening lines as a precise restaging of the ways in which the female "Mummum" ensheathes the expiring voice of the male "Ha he hi ho hu." The letter "t" that is linked to the male elements in the *Wake* dominates and regulates the rhythm of the predicative "tomtittot to teetootomtotalitarian," and its dominance of the phrase is marked as "totalitarian." In the following phrase, "Tea tea too oo," the play of the "t" is limited and then truncated by the technique of "caps ever"ing (*FW* 260.4).

This "caps ever"ing, or severing of the cap, or capital (the operation takes place in the severing of the "s" from "sever" and its grafting on to the end of "cap"), is a process of decapitalization Derrida elsewhere discusses within the context of the general economy of writing. Capitalization is a process by which capital (in both its economic and linguistic sense) can be stored up within the economy of writing. It guarantees the power of the proper name (of the book, the author, and, in phallocentric terms, of the Father) and its ability to dominate that economy. The process of de-

capitalizing is involved in writing's ability to ruin the proper name and limit its power.

This re-marking of the antiphallocentric process takes place as the capital of "Tea" is reduced to the lowercase of "tea" and the lowercase "t" of "too" is severed to produce the female "oo" that engages in a play with ALP's double, overlapping circles (293). It is a movement from the masculine proper name "tom" ("*tom*tittot," "teetoo*tom*totalitarian" [emphasis added]) to the female "oo." This simultaneous limitation and truncation of the masculine and the subsequent shift to the feminine mirror the shift through laughter from the masculine "Ha *he* hi ho hu" (emphasis added), in which a decapitalizing also takes place, to the female "Mummum" of the last section. At the same time, the passage also restages the subversion of the phallocentric central column of text in the lessons section. This movement against the power of the phallocentric is also echoed in the central column's exclamation, "Am shot, says the big-guard" (*FW* 260.6–7).

As Margot Norris's pioneering *The Decentered Universe of* Finnegans Wake (Norris 1974) first made clear, Joyce's writing operates according to the Freudian principles of condensation, displacement, and substitution. It also articulates the "either/or" grammatical construction (signifying a choice of alternatives at the conscious level) becoming (at the level of the unconscious) a signifier of conjunction. At the level of the unconscious, the formula "either/or = and" operates. This formula is set to work in the lessons passage, "Enten eller, either or. And!" (*FW* 281.26–28). Employing Freud's principle of negation, Joyce's writing takes this formula one step further by negating the "And" with "Nay" and then privileging pleasure and/or preference with "rather!":

> Enten eller,
> either or.
> And!   INTERROGATION.
> Nay, rather!   EXCLAMATION.
>   (*FW* 281.25–28)

This critique of phallogocentrism articulates a movement from the logocentric division between "either" and "or" to the conjunction of "and," and then, through the operation of "nay," rearticulates the principle of negation with which the conscious denies those pleasures that are the object of unconscious desire.

Removing the either/or distinction makes any final identification of gender extremely difficult, if not impossible, which is something Joyce's text already knows when it tells us that "in this scherzarade of one's thousand one nightinesses that sword of certainty which would indentifide the body never falls" (*FW* 51.4–5). While we can identify ALP as female and HCE as male, we have to remember that HCE is identified with a mountain and ALP with an "alp." While the *Wake* celebrates HCE and his erections like the "waalworth of a skyerscape" (*FW* 4.35–36) built by "Bygmester Finnegan" (4.18), it also articulates ALP's female language and the "gramma's grammar" (*FW* 268.17) with which Issy writes her letter.

Derrida identifies a paradox that explains this apparent (con)fusion of the masculine and feminine and the phallocentric and antiphallocentric in the *Wake:* "sometimes the texts which are the most phallocentric or phallogocentric in their themes . . . can also be, in some cases, the most deconstructive . . . There are sometimes more deconstructive resources . . . in some text by Joyce or Ponge, who are often phallocentric in appearance, than in some texts which, thematically, are theatrically 'feminist' or 'antiphallocentric,' be they signed by the names of men or women" (Derrida 1992b:58).

The *Wake* clearly has both phallocentric and antiphallocentric impulses. The reader can attempt to separate the two, but in so doing, he may be producing the results of a critical operation carried out under the restrictions of the logic of the either/or rather than re-marking the *Wake*'s (con)fusion of the two. Joyce's writing already says anything that we could possibly say about it. Any decisions that we make at the conscious level about either the phallocentrism or the antiphallocentrism of that writing will always already have been made and then set to work in that writing according to the formula of either/or = and. Ask Joyce's writing "Why?" and it gives answers to that question in a condensation of "I don't know," "because I am such," and "search me": "Why? Such me" (*FW* 597.22).

The powerful masculine voices that emerge in many places in the *Wake*'s complex circular narratives are frequently phallocentric. Derrida notes how the *Wake* "says 'we' and 'yes' . . . to the Father or to the Lord who speaks loud, there is scarcely anyone but Him, but it leaves the last word to the woman who in her turn will have said 'we' and 'yes'" (Derrida 1984a:158). The movement of this passage countersigns the antiphallocentric movements occurring elsewhere through Joyce's writing. The singularity of Joyce's feminine yes is doubled in the repetition of "mum," but this repetition is marked by a difference. The first "Mum" is capitalized; the second is decapitalized in the repetition, "mum." These "two [other] words for Joyce" complete the aphallocentric conversion from the male to the female through the laughter of "Ha he hi ho hu." They also countersign Joyce as an exemplar of Derrida's desire to allow the dissonance of speech to emerge from within the play of writing. After speaking these written words of Joyce in his "impromptu" discussion, Derrida allowed Joyce's writing and its haunting of his speech to be committed to the printed page and the safekeeping of the double, maternal, and silent positions signified by the English idiom of "keeping mum."

CHAPTER 8

Derrida's "Unde-cidables" (I)

A "Greeter Glossary" for Joyce's Codes

JOYCE'S WRITINGS ARE A POWERFUL revelation of the force of the doubles (writing, marks, binds, strategies, and so on) continually explored by Derrida. They practice deconstruction while simultaneously re-marking that practice theoretically. At the Ninth International James Joyce Symposium, Derrida said, "Deconstruction could not have been possible without Joyce" (Jones 1988:77). We have considered many of the sites, relays, and traces in Derrida's writings and talks that demonstrate Derrida has developed and maintained a strong interest in Joyce's writings, particularly in his last two works, and this evidence shows that Derrida sees the unrepeatable singularity of Joyce's work as one of the most powerful effects of his writings. This singularity is sustained by the double of Joyce's writing as literary *and* philosophical.

Although the word "perhaps" still hangs over Derrida's assessment of Joyce as the "most Hegelian of novelists," there is much to support the argument that Derrida finds Hegel's encyclopedic and totalizing philosophical project paralleled (or "completed") by Joyce's "most powerful project for programming . . . the totality of research in the onto-logico-encyclopedic field." For Derrida, readers and scholars who engage with Joyce's writings find themselves playing "with the entire archive of culture—at least of what is called Western culture, and, in it, of that which returns to itself according to the Ulyssean circle of the *encyclopedia*" (Derrida 1992a:281; emphasis added).

Like *Ulysses* and *Finnegans Wake,* Derrida's writings on Joyce (as well as his other writings) are structured by circularity and the notion of return. In the most straightforward statement on his deconstructive projects we have examined, Derrida states, "You know, in fact, that above all it is necessary to read and *reread* those in whose wake I write, the 'books' in whose margins and between whose lines I mark out and read a text simultaneously almost identical and entirely other" (Derrida 1987b:4; emphasis added). This process of rereading is a process of return. Derrida's returning to Joyce's work for more than thirty years reveals how strong both the return and the work are in Derrida's deconstructive project as a process of "interminable analysis" (Derrida 1987a:42).

Derrida uses the *Wake*'s metaphor of its language as a river to re-mark the continual return involved in such a rereading and to signify how returning to Joyce's work produces the effect of encountering that work anew each time. Discussing how naive and "irresistibly comical" it is to claim to have "read Joyce," Derrida explains that "you stay on the edge of reading Joyce . . . and the endless plunge throws you back onto the river-bank, on the brink of another possible immersion, *ad infinitum.* Is this true to the same extent of all works? In any case, I have the feeling that I haven't yet begun to read Joyce, and this 'not having begun to read' is sometimes the most singular and active relationship I have with this work" (Derrida 1984a: 148).

We have seen how a significant part of Derrida's project has been the production of texts that question and disturb traditional philosophical logic and the systems of binary opposition that govern the operations of that logic. Within his readings of both philosophical and literary texts, Derrida has developed numerous "certain marks" (for example, "différance," "gram," "trace," "spacing," "margin," "arche-writing," "the double," "incision," "blank") that "can no longer be included within philosophical (binary) opposition, but which . . . inhabit philosophical opposition, resisting and disorganizing it" (Derrida 1987b:43).

The following selective interrogation of Derrida's "undecidables" explores how they can be used to re-mark the deconstructive effects of Joyce's writing and their haunting of Derrida's work. Derrida uses the words *undecidable* and *nonconcept* to stress that the terms he lists under these names cannot be fully explained, nor their signifying play controlled, with traditional philosophical and literary concepts working under the laws of binary opposition. They operate in the same way as the word *pharmakos* in Plato's retelling of the myth of Theuth and Ammon Ra. Theuth "*turns* the word on its strange and visible pivot" (Derrida 1981:97).

Derrida emphasizes "turns" to open up a double, tropic play: *pharmakos* can be turned so that it signifies either *medicine* or *poison*. At the same time that *turn* emphasizes the ambivalence of this term, it also triggers the physical metaphor of the trope as a mechanical device that turns on a pivot. In this way, Derrida exceeds the binarism of simple ambiguity and draws attention to ways in which *turn* opens up a further chain of significations linked to his notion of a word as a "trigger" (Derrida 1981:290–96) that can set other signifying chains (and signifying chains of the text's "other") in motion.

A term like *gram* (which Derrida lists as one of his undecidables and designates "the most general concept of semiology—which thus becomes grammatology" [Derrida 1987b:26]) is put to work so that it exceeds binary opposition through the play of its multiple polysemous values. We have seen that, at a basic physical level, the term signifies the very process of inscription that leaves an inscribed mark on the page. This process not only creates and defines the gram but also brings into play the operations of the blank (another of Derrida's undecidables) spaces on either side of the mark. These white *(blanc)* spaces are double marks (another undecidable) that help define the gram at the same time they are created and brought into play by it. *Gram* can also signify letters and words, the *Wake*'s anagrams (or Anna's grams), as well as operate in some of the various technical terms (phonogram, telegram, gramophone) whose metaphoric values we have seen Derrida explore.

Finnegans Wake frequently foregrounds the textual operations signified by Derrida's undecidables and nonconcepts. Re-marking these operations in Joyce's writing with Derrida's terms also re-marks the return that Harold Bloom signifies with the use of the Greek word *apophrades* (Bloom 1973:141). This term refers to the return of the dead, and Bloom uses it to describe the ways in which a writer's precursors can return to haunt his work. It is therefore an appropriate term for the ways in which the spectral power of Joyce's writings returns to haunt Derrida's work. Derrida's formulation of his nonconcepts has been greatly influenced by his reading of Joyce and his re-marking of some of the textual effects of Joyce's writing. Using Derrida's terms to allow for a recognition of those effects as they operate within Joyce is little more than re-marking Joyce's texts with their own operations, or rendering unto Joyce's writing of what always already belonged to it.

Although the institutionalized deconstruction that Rodolphe Gasché describes as a form of New Criticism attempts a systematic textual analysis, Derrida's project cannot be summarized or "booked" into a formula or method (although this is frequently "done" in many studies of his work) any more than Joyce's writings can be fully explained by subsuming them under the taxonomic categories of plot, character, theme, motif, structure, diction, rhetoric, grammar or lexicon, and so on. Derrida consciously works "to bring the critical operation to bear against the unceasing reappropriation of this work of the simulacrum [another undecidable] by a dialectics of the Hegelian type . . . for Hegelian idealism consists precisely of a *relève* of the binary oppositions of classical idealism . . . while *interning* difference in a self-presence." The "undecideables" resist such reappropriation while "inhabit[ing] philosophical opposition." They resist and disorganize this opposition and its possible *relève* by never "constituting a third term" or "leaving room for a solution in the form of speculative dialectics (the *pharmakon* is neither remedy nor poison . . . the *gram* is neither a signifier nor a signified, neither a sign nor a thing, neither a presence nor an absence. . . . Neither/nor, that is, *simultaneously* either *or* . . .)" (Derrida 1987b:43).

The assertion that all writing is structured by *différance* is a generalization worthy of Blake's idiot. Yet even in writing that works to stifle and suppress the multisymbolic play of language in the dream of achieving a self-present, fullness of meaning, Derrida has detected and marked the effects of his analogous "undecidables." Joyce's writings enact the play of innumerable differences, and his writings, particularly *Finnegans Wake,* work toward revealing themselves as an ultimately undefinable process of becoming (in) language that will continually defeat our attempts at analyzing, defining, and appropriating it as a stable being, subject or object. Derrida shows how these analytic tools can be set aside as weapons of mastery in order to attend to some of their other functions (and their functions as the "other" in the linear model of the alterity of writing created by a limiting empirical historicism).

Stephen Dedalus wanted to escape the nets that he saw thrown up to prevent his flight from Ireland, but we cannot escape from or finish a reading of Joyce. We can, however, learn to dwell more comfortably in his writing by using the lessons on plurivocity and associative logic that it teaches. We can, for example, use the simple process of turning "nets" on its "invisible pole" to signify the tools we can dip into the river of Joyce's language in order to try and catch a glimpse of HCE as "erst crafty hakemouth" (*FW* 263.2), and, when we "have snakked mid [this] fish" (*FW* 597.36), we can return him safely into the water of the *Wake,* where he belongs.

As Derrida does in his writing, Joyce programs the element of chance into the "being" of his linguistic, encyclopedic project. In the terms of a divisive and defining analytic logic, it seems that no matter how "practical" or "predicable" we are, Joyce's writing as a "kind of being with a difference" will forever lie beyond the abilities of our analytic and interpretative strategies to master. The chance programmed into Joyce's writing, however, creates precisely the "proper sort of accident" we can and "must have" in order to "meet" (but not master) "that kind of being" (*FW* 269.14–15) that disappears in its own appearance within Joyce's continual play of difference and deferral.

With the sense of a Joycean mission impossible, the following glossary is offered as a chance for a deconstructive encounter with some selected samples from Joyce's writings. The choice of "undecidables" is random and necessarily incomplete because "by definition the list has no taxonomic closure, and even less does it constitute a lexicon" (Derrida 1987b:40). In the *Wake*'s radio broadcast, the "Ellers" (Da. "other"), or "others" for the "greeter glossary of code" (*FW* 324.21), exist both for the "greater glory of god"—which re-marks the Jesuit motto with which both Joyce and Stephen Dedalus were so familiar—as well as for the "greeter," who uses the glossary of radio codes to "callen hom" (*FW* 324.21), or "call home." The following glossary of Derrida's terms is a way of "greeting" Joyce's texts with some of the textual operations that are already at "home" there.

Many of the examples of Joyce's writing are from *Finnegans Wake,* because that text, more than any of Joyce's earlier texts, foregrounds itself as a practice of writing and frequently reminds us of its linguistic status as a writing *practice*. The examples of this foregrounding are well known and include the *Wake*'s reminder of the unusual nature of its language ("nat language at any sinse of the world" [*FW* 83.12]); the signification of the lines and graphic inscriptions of the text (the "ruled barriers along which the traced words, run, march, halt, walk, stumble at doubtful points" [*FW* 114.7–9]); and the reminder that language and its graphic elements are in themselves signatures ("So why, pray, sign any-thing as long as every word, letter, penstroke, paperspace is a perfect signature of its own?" [*FW* 115.6–8]).

Arche-writing

Arche-writing is not only an "undecidable"; like the *Wake,* it is also ulti-mately undefinable. There is little doubt, however, that Derrida sees the writing of *Finnegans Wake* as a powerful practice of arche-writing. The term suggests an ancient or "originary" writing, a writing that is already involved in, or necessary to, that natural, original (spoken) language that is supposed to precede and give its meaning to writing. At stake in the non-concept of arche-writing is the priority and privilege of speech (presence) over writing (absence) in Western metaphysics. Arche-writing resists and disorganizes such priority and privilege, thus putting in question the notion of "origin" itself, and the phenomenological concept of an origin un-touched by nonorigin, which constitutes it. Arche-writing is "that very thing which cannot let itself be reduced to the form of *presence*" (Derrida 1976:57).

In general terms, the operations of arche-writing can be equated with the play of *différance* and the operations of the trace. Although Derrida uses the term to signify a force that is at work "not only in the form and substance of graphic expression, but also in those of nongraphic expression" (Derrida 1976:60), he does not see it as a transcendental form. The difficulty of apprehending the operations of arche-writing is the difficulty of apprehend-ing the operations of the trace: it only appears in the process of its own disappearing.

One way of engaging with the operations of arche-writing in Joyce's texts is to attend to the ways in which his writing obliterates the proper name in a process of constitutive erasure. This is because arche-writing is continu-ally involved in the production and obliteration of the proper name: "the proper name was never possible except through its functioning within a classification and therefore within a system of differences, within a writing retaining the traces of difference" (Derrida 1976:109). As early as *Dub-liners,* Joyce offers us processes of constitutive erasure. In "Clay," for ex-ample, the "proper name" or title of the story, which signifies the substance Maria is given by the "next-door girls," never appears in the story itself. In *Ulysses* we have the constitutive erasures of the proper name in the numer-ous variations on "Bloom": "Bloo. . . . Me? No. Blood of the Lamb" (*U* 124); "Blew. Blue bloom is on the. . . . Jingle. Bloo. . . . I feel so sad. P.S. So lonely blooming" (*U* 210); "Bloowho" (*U* 212); "ben Bloom Elijah" (*U* 283); "*the new Bloomusalem*" (*U* 395).

Finnegans Wake offers countless examples of arche-writing ruining the proper name. Even Joyce's well-known desire to outwrite Shakespeare provides examples of how Joyce was able to attempt this impossible project by ruining the proper name of his potential rival. Shakespeare's name never appears in its "proper" form within the *Wake* and the various deformations that signify the playwright ("Shapesphere" [*FW* 295.4], "shaggspick" [*FW* 177.32], "Shakefork" [*FW* 274.L4], "shakespill" [*FW* 161.31], "Shakhisbeard" [*FW* 177.32]) simultaneously erase and ruin his proper name even as they constitute a signifier of it. Joyce of course was quite willing to allow his writing to ruin his own proper name, and although his name appears on the spine and the title page of the *Wake,* within the text it appears only as simultaneously erasing and constitutive puns.

The Blank (and Whites and the Hymen)

The theories of the blank are developed most fully in *Dissemination*'s "The Double Session," where Derrida explores Mallarmé's *Mimique.* His exploration of the blank is grounded in the white *(blanc)* pages of the book on which writing takes place, but it quickly unfolds into a series of analogies and metaphors for the operations of writing. Besides the blank, white page waiting for inscription, the blank is also the "white face" of the mime whose face is like a blank page inscribed only with the trace of a tear. At the same time, the blank is analogous with the hymen, and the inscription of the pen "proceeds without a past upon [this] virgin sheet" (Derrida 1981:223). Under the heading of a general concept of writing inclusive of other forms of art, Derrida contends, "literature, theatre, drama, ballet, dance, fable and mimicry are forms of writing that are subject to the law of the hymen" (Derrida 1981:242).

This law of the hymen determines that representation and mimesis will be no more than one value amongst a series of valences. The blank is the scene of writing; but while it is more than the blank page on which writing is inscribed, it also has its limits: although the "blank or the whiteness (is) the totality, however infinite, of the polysemic series, *plus* the carefully spaced-out splitting of the whole, . . . it is not *The* blank proper, [or a] transcendental origin of the series." As one example of the blank (amongst many others), the "whiteness of the page of writing" cannot and should not be erected "into the fundamental signified or signifier of the series." This is a "common law," and every "signifier in the series is folded along the angle of [its] remark" (Derrida 1981:252).

"The signifiers 'writing,' 'hymen,' 'fold,' 'tissue,' 'text,' etc., do not escape this common law, and only a common conceptual strategy of some sort can temporarily privilege them as *determinate* signifiers or even as *signifiers* at all, which strictly speaking they *no longer are*" (Derrida 1981:252). The endless play of the blanks and the white spaces forces thematic criticism to its limits. The theme and meanings of the blanks and white spaces "cannot ... be mastered," and when we realize "it is within the folds and blankness of a certain hymen that the very textuality of the text is re-marked, then we will precisely have determined the limits of thematic criticism itself" (Derrida 1981:245–46).

An analysis of the blank as it unfolds in Joyce's writing (while it simultaneously re-marks the play and rhythm of that writing) might begin with the *Wake*'s signification of the "paperspace" as a "perfect signature of its own" (*FW* 115.7–8) and then continue by analyzing the other places in which the blank is re-marked. These would include the blank page(s) upon which Issy writes her letter and the twins inscribe the diagram of the maternal vagina in their lessons. We have seen how the *blanc* of Joyce's "paperspace" operates as the marginal spaces from which the assault is launched upon the central, phallic column of text in that section. On the final page of the lessons section, the central column is limited and demarcated precisely by the white spaces between the left-and right-hand margins and itself. Derrida's theory of the blanks also provides a way to explore the numerous places in which the *Wake* draws attention to its own spacing in passages such as "B—y b—r's" (*FW* 81.26) or "A . . . .! ? . . . . O!" (*FW* 94.21–22), the latter re-marking the limits of both the Greek alphabet and the Christian God as the alpha and omega, or beginning and end, within philosophical and theological theories of existence.

The ability of typographic blanks to regulate the play of meaning is evident in the effect of the spaces marking the omissions in Old Cotter's speech in "The Sisters." These blanks hint at a taboo, something that must remain outside the boundaries of speech and something that the adults consider as inappropriate knowledge for the boy. They simultaneously signify both the boy's lack of understanding of what has happened to him and the nature of the priest's unspeakable (and undefinable) transgression.

At a metaphoric level, the blank allows for an analysis of the boy's interest in the "lighted square of window" (*D* 1), where he looks for some sign of the priest's death. The textual functions of the blank simultaneously conceal and reveal the actions of the pervert whom the boys meet in "An Encounter": what the man does between his double speeches of seduction and chastisement are signified by a gap in the text that is marked by Mahoney's "I say! Look what he's doing" (*D* 18). We can guess that the man might be masturbating, but the blank conceals his actions from us while simultaneously making our guess possible.

The metaphoric and metonymic play of the blank is at work in the window curtains against which Eveline lays her head as well as in the "indistinct" and indecipherable "white of two letters in her lap" (*D* 32). One could explore the constellation of the blanks as they regulate the polysemy of *Dubliners*. This would allow for the gathering together of the nameless characters (as in "The Sisters," "An Encounter," "Araby," or the woman in "Two Gallants") and an analysis of what is signified by the lack of identity as a lack created by the ruining of the proper name in Joyce's writing. The lack of any clear identification of the central events in some of the stories also creates a series of textual blanks: What does the priest do to the boy in "The Sisters"? What does the man do in "An Encounter"? Why does the quest fail in "Araby"? Does Bob Doran remain a celibate? What is the "mystery" behind Richard Tierney's religious and financial status in "Ivy Day in the Committee Room"? The operations of such blanks regulate the rhythmic, textual play of *Dubliners* from the missing hope ("There was no hope for him this time" [*D* 1]) that opens the collection to the uncertain future and "last end" (*D* 225) of Gretta and Gabriel, which lies buried within the play of the whites, as Michael Furey, and all of Ireland, lies buried beneath the snow.

Within the textual blank or hymen, Derrida discovers a "fold" re-marking the limits of language's mimetic play. This fold is constituted by the supplementary relation of the "blank," which "marks everything white" (like the snow at the end of "The Dead"), and the "blankness that allows for the mark in the first place." The latter is a supplement in that it "comes neither before nor after" the former and can be subtracted from the series of blanks marking everything white "(in which case it is determined as a lack to be silently passed over)" or added "as an extra number to the series" (Derrida 1981:253). The (supplementary) fold prevents the play of language from being limited by its mimetic function: "If there is no such thing as a total or proper meaning, it is because the blank *folds over*" (Derrida 1981:258). "According to the structure of supplementarity, what is added is thus always a blank or a fold: the fact of addition gives way to a kind of multiple division or subtraction that enriches itself with zeros as it races breathlessly toward the infinite" (Derrida 1981:262). There can be no total meaning, no total representation or mimesis in this play of possibly infinite substitutions and supplementations of the blank.

In *Ulysses,* the limitations of language's mimetic function are marked within just such folded and enfolding blanks. This can be seen in the operations of the advertising slogan for Plumtree's potted meat, placed on one side of the blank space beneath the death notices in the *Freeman's Journal,* which we first encounter when, during his meeting with M'Coy, Bloom "unrolled the newspaper baton idly and read idly: *What is home without Plumtree's Potted Meat? Incomplete. With it an abode of bliss*" (*U* 61). This slogan remains in Bloom's mind as he walks through Dublin, and, when he enters Davey Byrne's, Bloom's meditations produce a series of "potted meats" linking the slogan with necrophagy: "Potted meats. What is home without Plumtree's potted meat? Incomplete. What a stupid ad! Under the obituary notices they stuck it. All up a plumtree. Dignam's potted meat. Cannibals would with lemon and rice" (*U* 140). This series is sustained by a "blank" for the constituting link, which would be the verb *to eat,* is lacking, passed over: "Cannibals would [blank] with lemon and rice."

When we first encounter a jar of potted meat (as opposed to its "representation" in the slogan), it is as a blank, and we do not know exactly what the object is. While Boylan is purchasing the phallic present of the bottle of port, "fat pears" and "ripe shamefaced peaches" in the "bedded" wicker basket that he will have sent to Molly, he gives the shop assistant in Thornton's the bottle of port "swathed in pink tissue paper and a *small jar*" (*U* 187; emphasis added). We can guess at the identity of this "small jar" only after the textual detective work made possible by a retroactive rereading of the passage. The "Ithaca" section provides a series of the items that "lay under exposure" on the "shelves of the kitchen dresser, opened by Bloom" (*U* 551). Listed among the items in this series are "an empty pot of Plumtree's potted meat, an oval wicker basket bedded with fibre and containing one Jersey pear, a halfempty bottle of William Gilbey and Co's white invalid port, half disrobed of its swathe of coralpink tissue paper" (*U* 552). The effect of this exposure, via the blank, is that potted meat now also operates in another series of signs, this time the series signifying sexual activity.

The sexual signification of potted meat is confirmed when Bloom climbs into bed next to Molly: "his limbs, when gradually extended, encounter. . . . New clean bedlinen, additional odours, the presence of a human form, female, hers, the imprint of a human form, male, not his, some crumbs, some flakes of potted meat, recooked, which he removed" (*U* 601). These "flakes" are traces signifying that Boylan and Molly have shared their "potted meat" in bed, and they confirm the identity of the small jar Boylan asks the girl in Thornton's to put in the basket with the port and peaches. At the same time, the crumbs and flakes that Bloom discovers on the whites of the "clean bedlinen" are signifiers bearing witness to, and re-marking, the sexual activities that may have transpired that afternoon in the Blooms's bed. These events themselves are then entered into another supplementary series. Bloom's subsequent reflection, after he has "removed" the traces from the sheets (which he is now re-marking himself), is an articulation of supplementarity itself: "To reflect that each one who enters imagines himself to be the first to enter whereas he is always the last term of a preceding series even if the first term of a succeeding one, each imagining himself to be first, last, only and alone whereas he is neither first nor last nor only nor alone in a series originating in and repeated to infinity" (U 601).

Before this final appearance of the potted meat, a textual blank opens up spaces between the jar of potted meat, its representation in the language of the advertising slogan and the insertion of the slogan in the newspaper. Earlier in the "Ithaca" section, the narrator ironically asks what things had "never" (U 560) "stimulated" Bloom "in his cogitations" (U 559). The response is the advertising slogan and a potted history of the meat's production: "What is home without Plumtree's Potted Meat? Incomplete. With it an abode of bliss. Manufactured by George Plumtree, 23 Merchants' quay, Dublin, put up in 4 oz pots, and inserted by Councillor Joseph P. Nannetti, M.P., Rotunda Ward, 19 Hardwicke street, under the obituary notices and anniversaries of deceases" (U 560). The history of the production of potted meat, which follows the slogan, folds back to re-mark both the meat and the pot in which it is contained, as well as the slogan with which it is represented. At this point in the text, another space, or blank, opens up between the objects of the meat, the pots and their representation in the slogan that is "inserted" in the newspaper.

The parallel phrases beginning with "Manufactured" and "inserted" should, but do not, share the same referent. The distance between them produces a space that re-marks the limitations of mimesis, or representation. The shared grammatical referents for "Manufactured" and "inserted" are the meat and the pots (and the movement from the singular meat to the plural pots re-marks another doubling), but the pot can be "inserted" in the newspaper only through mimesis. Joyce's text knows this fact, and, following the summary of the production of the potted meat, it exploits a copyright cliché in order to mark the limitations of naming and mimesis: "The name on the label is Plumtree. A plumtree in a meatpot, registered trade mark. *Beware of imitations*" (U 560; emphasis added). Following this warning about the limitations of imitation, the text reveals how writing can ruin the proper name and mimesis can fail: "Peatmot. Trumplee. Moutpat. Plamtroo" (U 560).

The Book as an Ideological Structure

The stories from *Dubliners* are clearly analyzable with the traditional, tripartite Aristotelian plot structure. Their narratives can be divided in this way, but, along with a considerable number of other modernist texts, they challenge the notion that a literary story should have a plot leading toward a climax that will bring the action(s) to a head and a subsequent denouement offering some kind of resolution. Joyce's stories lack a center and offer a vision of an existence that is decentered. In "The Boarding House," for example, the event that would function as the center of a traditional plot is missing. We see Bob Doran lighting Polly's candle, but the two times Doran is described as a celibate make it unclear if Doran actually did what Mrs. Mooney will accuse him of. (Her accusations are clearly hinted at, but we do not witness her discussion with Doran.)

The structures of *A Portrait of the Artist as a Young Man* have been explored in depth by many critics, yet it is still worth considering how some of their conclusions can be reconsidered within the context of Joyce's deconstruction of the ideology of the model of the literary book. There is the well-known ambiguity making it impossible to decide if Stephen is being depicted as an artist or only as a young man who has yet to become one. Although his one adolescent poem suggests the latter, the title remains ambiguous, and a reading of the text must work between the undecidable double created by the two choices.

By including a mixture of third-person and omniscient perspective in the narrative and combining this in a bricolage that gathers a simulacrum of baby talk, dialogue, catechism, poetry, a sermon, and a philosophic disquisition on aesthetics, Joyce breaks with the traditional literary concept of a unified and totalizing style. The irregular diary entries in the present tense at the end of the book complete that break, and, instead of concluding the novel, they offer the invocation to the Dedalus of Greek myth after Stephen marks his future in the continuous present tense: "I go to encounter for the millionth time the reality of experience" (*PA* 275–76).

From Derrida's perspective, what Joyce achieves in *Portrait* is the creation of a "grouped textual field" that is the only site from which deconstruction can take place (Derrida 1987b:42). Instead of a regular and "punctual position" afforded by a single narrator, *Portrait* offers a shifting series of texts signed by different narrators: the stories by Simon Dedalus, Dante, and Uncle Charles; the poem by Dante; the sermon by the rector; the narrative by Davin; the disquisition on the tundish by the dean of studies;

and Stephen's lecture on applied Aquinas. Joyce countersigns all these narratives, but they are signed within the text by the characters to whom they are attributed.

Joyce is of course not alone in participating in the destruction of the form of the book as that form was understood by many of his predecessors. As Derrida notes, this destruction gets "underway in all domains." It is, nevertheless, a destruction that Joyce continues to pursue in his later works. It is not a negative destruction, but one that positively "denudes the surface of the text" and allows the operations of the text to be foregrounded (Derrida 1976:18).

We have considered how the *Wake* undermines the ideology of the book, and the next chapter considers how both *Ulysses* and the *Wake* participate in this subversion. The deconstructive context for Joyce's assault on traditional literary forms and the ideology of the book is a positive one that allows for a lifting of the linearity involved in the "repression of pluridimensional symbolic thought" (Derrida 1976:86). *Ulysses* and *Finnegans Wake* are both epics, but they are epics with a difference. They are two of the many "shocks that are gradually destroying the linear model [of the book, of thinking, of writing, etc.]. Which is to say the *epic* model." What Derrida says of the attempt to write what is thought by deconstruction applies equally to the attempt at understanding Joyce with linear concepts about books, literature, and writing: it cannot be done "except by imitating the operation implicit in teaching modern mathematics with an abacus" (Derrida 1976:87).

CHAPTER 9

Undecidables (II)

Deconstruction and the
Différance of Joyce

Différance IS PERHAPS THE MOST WELL
known of Derrida's undecidables. We have examined how this neologism is
a (con)fusion of *defer* and *differ* that signifies the ways in which meaning is
made possible by the very differences (of, and between, letters, spaces, punctuation, sounds, and silences) that sustain desire while deferring its ultimate
object. Derrida finds différance operating at all levels of writing: in the
different graphic marks (letters, spacing, punctuation marks, accent marks)
that make writing intelligible; in the differences between words (within one
language but also between the different words for the same objects and
concepts from different languages); in the differences between signifiers and
their signifieds; in the spaces between the terms of binary opposition that
govern and control the operations of philosophical logic; in the operations
of arche-writing; and in the operations of the trace. The term signifies not
only the differences that structure language and make its operations possible, but also (and simultaneously) the deferral of meaning that accompa-
nies all linguistic operations.

Even the self-presence of interior thought is structured by difference and a deferral of meaning. Derrida questions and solicits the classical hierarchy that privileges thought over speech and speech over writing on the basis of presence. The notion that the interiority of thought can guarantee a presence (of meaning, of ideas and concepts) that speech cannot guarantee is for Derrida an illusory notion, and the idea that speech can provide a presence (of the speaker and the listener, of meaning, of intention) that writing cannot is misleading.

If it were possible to speak of the structure of deconstruction, it would be tempting to say that *différance* is at the center of Derrida's project. As this is not possible, it may be sufficient to note how powerful this "nonconcept" is in the deconstruction of the binary oppositions Derrida sees as one of the prominent features of logocentric and phallogocentric thought. Derrida has said that "if there were a definition of *différance,* it would be precisely the limit, the interruption, the destruction of the Hegelian *relève wherever it operates*" (Derrida 1987b:40). This *relève* signifies that part of the Hegelian dialectical *aufhebung,* or sublation, by which the antithesis is lifted up into the interiority of the thesis and remarked with its own negativity.

It is important to recall how the project of deconstruction gets under way by marking the difference and deferral that exist between the terms of binary opposition and make possible the privileging of one term over the other. It is imperative to "recognize that in a classical philosophical opposition we are not dealing with the peaceful coexistence of a *vis-à-vis,* but rather with a violent hierarchy." Within the opposition, "one of the two terms governs the other (axiologically, logically, etc.), or has the upper hand" (Derrida 1987b:41). After the difference and deferral structuring the opposition are re-marked, then the terms are overturned in a phase that must be part of an "interminable analysis" because "the hierarchy of dual oppositions always re-establishes itself" (Derrida 1987b:42).

The second part of deconstruction's "double writing" and "double science" "must . . . mark the interval between [the] inversion [the overturning], which brings low what was high, and the irruptive emergence of a new 'concept,' a concept that can no longer be, and never could be, included in the previous regime." This interval is a "biface or biphase" and can only "be inscribed . . . in a bifurcated writing," or what Derrida also terms a "grouped textual field" (Derrida 1987b:42). The example that Derrida uses for this deconstructive, double overturning reveals the importance of différance as a signifier of the deconstruction of the classical hierarchy that privileges speech over writing. The bifurcated writing that makes deconstruction possible "holds first of all for a new concept of writing, that *simultaneously* provokes the overturning of the hierarchy speech/writing, and the entire system attached to it, *and* releases the dissonance of a writing within speech, thereby disorganizing the entire inherited order and invading the entire field" (Derrida 1987b:42).

The *a* with which Derrida replaces the second *e* in difference is a graphic distinction, and in French *différence* is pronounced the same as *différance*. Derrida points out that "this graphic difference (*a* instead of *e*), this marked difference between two apparently vocal notations, between two vowels, remains purely graphic: it is read, or it is written, but it cannot be heard. It cannot be apprehended in speech" (Derrida 1982:3). Derrida thus reveals that written language is capable of a subtle distinction that cannot be detected in speech. This concern with the relationships between speech and writing is a powerful force in Derrida's continuing interest in Joyce and his admiration for Joyce's achievements. Joyce's own interest in the ways in which writing operates as a record of written speech is reflected by his decision not to use the inverted, double commas with which speech is traditionally represented in writing, and in *Finnegans Wake,* Joyce sets writing to work in a way that makes much of it unspeakable.

One of the effects of the *Wake*'s writing is what Stephen Heath terms an "optical listen." Of the perception that the *Wake* "is a book to be heard rather than read," Heath says "nothing could be more false." Using the pun on "for instance" ("for inkstands" [*FW* 173.34]) as an example, Heath explains that "no reading aloud could possibly pass 'for inkstands' and 'for instance' together" and that "the reading must choose." At the same time, any "reading of the text on the page" must consider all possible pronunciations available through the terms of the pun. In a reading of "for inkstands," the pronunciation of "for instance" must be considered and taken into account as a part of the written "for inkstands" (Heath 1984:58). In this way, the possible vocalization, the "speech form," of the pun is set to work, but only as a secondary force in the play of the pun's written or printed form. Like Derrida's différance, the puns of the *Wake* make written or printed language capable of a greater linguistic power to signify than the spoken forms it incorporates within itself. A great deal of Derrida's interest in the *Wake* is a result of the fact that Joyce's text is a written "being with a difference" (*FW* 269.15) that can also be read as a deconstructing being of différance, whose language constrains and limits the vocal elements of language in order to set them to work within writing.

Double ("Doublin") Marks

Derrida sets the concepts of the double mark and the double bind to work throughout his writing, and we have seen how Derrida's admiration of Joyce is linked to Joyce's status as a major creator and practitioner of the double in writing. For Derrida, double marks include the graphic marks that punctuate citation and "spoken" language in the written text; the double marks of parentheses and brackets; and the double dashes punctuating parenthetical phrases and clauses. On another level (which is also the level of the "other"), Derrida uses the double to investigate the relationship between the original, or model, and its imitation as that imitation is produced by the process of mimesis defined by Plato.

Mimesis produces the double of an (original) model that functions as a supplement that can stand next to the original and threaten to take its place. The space created by the double of the copy and the original is a space in which Derrida consciously situates much of his own writing, and, as we have already seen, it is a space that *Ulysses* opens up and explores as the space between meat, the pot that contains it, and their insertion in language through mimesis or imitation.

As many critics of Joyce have noted, *Ulysses* is a book of doubles, and many of the characters play at least a double role. Harold Bloom shows how *Ulysses* is founded "simultaneously upon the *Odyssey* and *Hamlet*" (Bloom 1994:414). Stephen Dedalus is a would-be writer, Hamlet, Telemachus, and a twentieth-century youth in search of a symbolic father; Bloom symbolically plays that father, the ghost of old Hamlet, the role of Odysseus, and the advertising salesman who is married to Molly. Molly is the Dublin singer and spouse to Bloom as well as Penelope and Boylan's lover. The plot is that of the story of *The Odyssey and* of a day in the lives of a singer, a failed writer, and an advertising salesman. The discourse of Molly's narrative makes it is possible to read *Ulysses* as a text with double endings. The first end comes with Bloom falling asleep and is punctuated with the enlarged dot that operates as a full stop to the adventures of Bloom and Dedalus as well as to the consciousness of Bloom; the second, with Molly's ultimate "Yes."

It is the *Wake* in which Joyce achieves most fully his mastery of the double, and it is that text which comes closest to a model for Derrida's deconstructing, bifurcated writing. One way of reading the *Wake* is to follow its chain of significations as they enact and sustain a seemingly endless process of bifurcation. This would be a similar process to that mapped out by Umberto Eco in "The Semantics of Metaphor," but instead of tracing the network of "subjacent metonymies" (Eco 1979:74–76) supporting the text's metaphors and puns, it would attend to the subtle changes by which a particular word is altered in order to extend the play of its signification while simultaneously maintaining a signifying play with its unaltered form.

Joyce's writing operates in the doubled and doubling textual spaces between mimesis and the disruption of it. On a mimetic level, much of the *Wake* is *about* events taking place in Dublin even as Joyce turns that city into his version of a universal city. One of the ways in which Joyce turns Dublin into a universal city is through a process signified in the text by a minimal alteration to the city's proper name (a process that disrupts and "ruins" that proper name and reveals the operations of the *Wake*'s archewriting). As his letter to Harriet Shaw Weaver reveals, Joyce "doubles" Dublin, Ireland, with the Dublin of Laurens Co., Georgia, the city founded by the ex-Dubliner Peter Sawyer (McHugh 1980:3). This process is an initial step in triggering a chain of bifurcation, and it is re-marked in the text by the decapitalization of "Dublin" to "dublin" and the insertion of an "o" into the word so that it gains the signification of "doublin," or "doubling": like the "topsawyer's rocks by the stream Oconee" (*FW* 3.7), certain words, or parts of them, become textual particles or "etyms" that can be seen "doublin their mumper all the time" (*FW* 3.8–9) and "doubling" their "number" "all the time."

The well-known pun describing the text as the "book of Doublends Jined" (*FW* 20.15–16) marks another step in this process of bifurcating, doubling (and Dublin) writing, and one self-reflectively re-marking the fundamental double structure of the text's double ends that can be linked by the reader. This same doubling process identifies HCE as the "doublejoynted janitor" (*FW* 27.2–3) who is the "janitor" and progenitor of Kevin and Jerry (who are doubles of Shem and Shaun); it brings London into play as a negative double of Dublin through the tale of Dick Whittington ("lode mere of Doubtlynn" [*FW* 248.7]); it describes HCE's cod piece (and shirt) as the "peascod doublet" (*FW* 578.8) that must have been removed when the phallic "phall" (*FW* 4.15) took place; and it draws our attention to the double lives, or "doublin existents" (*FW* 578.14), that HCE leads as an inhabitant of Dublin and a textual figure as well as a "daysent" (*FW* 578.14), or "decent," man and one who encounters his not-so-decent transgressions in his dreams.

This foregrounded doubling process is involved in the twin's drawing of ALP's "doubling bicirculars" (*FW* 295.31) and the subsequent urination that could take place in the "doubleviewed seeds" (*FW* 296.1), or WCs. At any point in the text's bifurcating network, the associative logic governing the simultaneous similarities and differences of Joyce's phonetic and/or graphic signifiers makes it possible to traverse the chains of metonymy supporting the *Wake*'s metaphors and puns to another section of text. From ALP's "bicirculars" one can follow the *Wake*'s "bi-furking" (*FW* 302.15–16) network through the metonymic links between "bi," or divided into two, and "bisect" in order to arrive at the topography of Phoenix Park and the "straight road" that "*bisexes* the park" (*FW* 564.10–11; emphasis added). One could just as easily take the same starting point and follow the metonymic chain of "bi," "divided into two," "two," "double," and re-arrive back at "Doublends Jined," which is itself another trope for "bicirculars." It is the rapidity with which the *Wake* makes such connections that Derrida emphasizes in his comparison of "the current technology of our computers" as "a *bricolage* of a prehistoric child's toy" with the "quasi-infinite speed and movements on Joyce's cables." "How," he asks, "could you calculate the speed with which a mark, a marked piece of information, is placed in contact with another in the same word or from one end of the book to the other?" (Derrida 1984a:147).

These double and doubling strategies Derrida explores (but which are always already set to work by Joyce) afford the opportunity of attending to the ways in which translation produces an (imperfect) double of a word or concept as that word or concept is translated from one language to another. With its raiding of the numerous languages that Joyce plundered, the *Wake* is a model and practical exercise in working within what Derrida calls the "double bind" of translation. One of Derrida's questions about Joyce is "How many languages can be lodged in two words by Joyce, lodged or inscribed, kept or burned, celebrated or violated?" (Derrida 1984a:145). Translation, as we saw earlier, is a double bind because an ideal translation is not possible. At best, translation can produce only an approximation of the meaning rendered by the original language. Many of the idioms and nuances of one language will always be lost in the translation into another language.

Derrida explores the impossible necessity of translation in numerous places. In *Dissemination* he focuses, as we have seen, on translations from Greek to Latin and from Latin into modern European languages. These two major translations constitute two "crucial hinges of Western philosophy: the textual rifts and drifts produced by the process of *translation* of the Greek philosophers, precisely, into Latin" (Derrida 1981:182 n. 10) and the translation of Greek and Latin thought into modern languages. In "Of an Apocalyptic Tone Recently Adopted in Philosophy," Derrida explores the double bind of translation in a context more relevant to his interest in Joyce.

This is the translation that humanity is forced to practice after the attempt to build the Tower of Babel is confounded by the Old Testament God. Derrida explains this double bind as this: "We must translate and we must not translate. I am thinking of the *double bind* of YHWH when, with the name of his choice, with the name one could say, Babel, he gives us *to translate and not to translate*. And no one, forever, since then, eludes the double postulation" (Derrida 1984b:3).

The mythemes of the Tower of Babel are interwoven with the *Wake*'s account of the falls of Finnegan and HCE throughout the text, and we have already seen how Joyce's use of them is a powerful attraction for Derrida. At the same time, the *Wake* also challenges its readers by forcing them to occupy the double bind of translation even when dealing only with the text's base language of English. To comprehend the various semantic values that Joyce (con)fuses in his puns, it is necessary to "translate" those values back into their original forms. In translating one of the puns generated by the Dublin/doubling pun, for example, it is necessary to identify the basic semantic elements that Joyce has fused together. One of the puns generated from that chain is "Dyoublong," and the text poses the question "So this is Dyoublong?" (*FW* 13.4). As the text is mapping out a visit to Dublin at this point, "Dublin" is obviously one of the primary semantic values at work in the pun. At the same time, the text is posing a question that one of the narrative voices is asking of another and, simultaneously, asking the same question of the reader.

To understand the question, it is necessary to translate "Dyoublong?" back into "Do you belong?" The double bind is that once the reader has translated the question into a more readily comprehensible form, then he is no longer reading Joyce's text but the results of an operation that he has performed upon it. The problem is more evident in a complex pun like "the maymeaminning of maimoomeining" (*FW* 267.3). Roland McHugh explicates this pun on the title of Ogden and Richard's book, *The Meaning of Meaning,* and teases out the semantic values of "opinion" (Ger. "meinung"), "love" (Ger. "minne"), and stuttering (I. meann, minne), and identifies the song title, "The Young May Moon" (McHugh 1980:267). There also may be the additional semantic values of "may," "me," "am," "mine" (L. "mea"), and "wound" ("maim") at work in the pun, as well as the onomatopoeic "moo" that would trigger a pun on the children's nursery rhyme about the cow that "jumped over the moon."

The number of possible semantic values the reader can demonstrate as operating within this pun will have no effect on the pun as it is defined by the term preceding it in the text: it is a scene of multiple imitations, or a "multimimetica" (FW 267.2–3) site, and in order to test if the possible semantic values are at work in the pun, the reader must again translate each "*etym*" (FW 353.22) of the pun into a comprehensible form. In so doing, however, the reader will be forced to occupy the double bind that determines translation as a necessary impossibility. Joyce's careful and painstaking construction of his puns can offer some hints about the operation of those puns (as a scene of multiple mimesis, or "multimimetica," for example), but it also forces the reader to realize that in order to understand many of the puns, it is necessary to go outside of the *Wake* to uncover the semantic values at work in the puns within it. This requires an erasure, or at least a temporary suspension, of the boundaries between the inside and the outside of the *Wake* to discover the external semantic values and sound plays Joyce has grafted into his writing.

Grafting

The "graft" is one of the eleven textual mechanisms Derrida explores in "Dissemination," where he links grafting with writing in a radical and fundamental way: "That is how the thing is written. To write means to graft. It's the same word" (Derrida 1981:355). The process of writing entails an incision (of a letter, a word, a phrase, or a larger sequence of words) from one text (the alphabet, a dictionary, a text that a writer wishes to "cite") and a subsequent grafting of the linguistic scion onto the new text. It can refer to the processes of quoting and citing and allows for close attention to the material, physical processes (as well as the mental processes) entailed in inscription and the transfer of inscribed (or printed) marks from one textual site to another.

Derrida's reading of *James Joyce's Scribbledehobble: The Ur-Workbook for* Finnegans Wake (Connolly 1961) attests to his interest in Joyce's processes of grafting: the citations, combinations, and accretions by which Joyce made entries in his notebooks and then transferred these entries, combining them and building up a palimpsest, into a subsequent draft for a particular passage of the *Wake*. Derrida explains that *Scribble,* his "partial translation" and introduction to Warburton's essay on hieroglyphics (book 4, section 4 of *The Divine Legation of Moses Demonstrated*) "constantly refer[s], . . . beyond even the title and the quotations" to *James Joyce's Scribbledehobble*" (Derrida 1984a:150). Derrida's title exemplifies this process of grafting by which the scion, "Scribble," is cut from its original site and grafted onto the title of Derrida's essay in such a way that it "continues to radiate back toward the site of its removal, transforming that, too, as it affects the new territory" (Derrida 1981:355).

Shortly after the visit to the museyroom in *Finnegans Wake,* Biddy appears as "a parody's bird" (*FW* 11.9), and the pun on "parody" and "paradise" makes her title signify and radiate back toward the numerous narrative sites of the prelapsarian paradise from which HCE and "Humpty shell fall frumpty times" (*FW* 12.12–13), or "shall fall umpteen times." This narrative loop includes the explanation that there are "two sights [as well as "sites" and "cites"] for ever a picture" (*FW* 11.36) and every picture. These "sights," "sites," and "cites" are created by the process of citing in a written, mimetic (and miming) language wherein "English might be seen" but "silence speaks the scene" (*FW* 13.1, 3). It creates the linguistic world of a "cell for citters to cit in" (*FW* 12.2), and one of the ways to feel at home in this strange world is to learn sitting as citing and citing as sighting, or seeing (which is also "theorizing"), to learn, in other words, how to re-cite, re-site, and re-sight, or look again, at the complex sites and scenes of this vastly complex, Dublin (and "doublin") city of a "citie" (*FW* 17.21).

The Gram (and Grammatology)

Related to the English terms *grammar* and *grave* (as in *engrave*), *gram* derives from a classical Greek term for *scratch* and is used in forms such as "having scratched marks or figures on a table"; "to draw lines with a pencil, to sketch, draw, paint"; and "to write" (*Liddell and Scott*). The term is also applicable to the rules of grammar and operates in the Greek phrase "to write down a law" (*Liddell and Scott*). In the previous chapter we saw how Derrida uses this term as one of his undecidables. At various times, he sets each of its semantic values to work in his writing.

At a fundamental physical level, even the simple inscription of a gram, or mark, on a blank page triggers the operations of the double of writing. Inscribing the mark, or gram, allows it to signify and simultaneously sets off the operations of the blank spaces that help to both define and limit the play of the mark that is in turn defined by them. *Of Grammatology* is Derrida's attempt to investigate the possibility of establishing a positive science of writing. It analyzes some of the general effects of the gram. These effects include that of the initial incision with which any mark is inscribed or engraved (including the initial letter of words or phrases) as well as the signifying operations triggered by such inscription and the rules and principles of such signification.

Of Grammatology investigates Western systems of phonetic writing with their supposed one-to-one relationships between the inscribed mark and its phonetic realization. These relationships are in contrast to those of Eastern, ideogrammatic systems of writing wherein the primary relationship is between the inscribed mark and the idea (rather than the sound) that it represents. The Western stress on the inscribed mark, letter, or word and the sound that it represents is signified by the term *phonocentrism,* which is related to (but not identical with) the terms of *logocentrism* and *phallocentrism,* as well as to the compound term *phallogocentrism.* These are, of course, terms that have become a familiar part of academic discourse precisely because of the dissemination of Derrida's theories of deconstruction.

We have already considered the force and play of the gram's operations in *Ulysses* and particularly the play of the "techne" of the gram, or the operations of the gramme within a technological mode (the telegram, the gram(s) inscribed on the postcards and transported through the postal system, the printed marks of newspapers, the marks Bloom scratches in the sand, the telephone as a sort of phonegram, and, of course, the gramophone). *Finnegans Wake* tells us that even the gram of a simple "penstroke" (as well as the blank of the "paperspace" that helps define it and regulate its play) is "a perfect signature all of its own" (*FW* 115.7–8), and one of the *Wake*'s numerous circular patterns traces the operations of the scratch, the inscribed mark, pen strokes, and other forms of the gram.

We considered some of these tracings by looking at the *Wake*'s references to its letters, words, and phrases, and the text's metonymic description of itself as a letter "uttered for Alp" (*FW* 420.18) allows us to read the various specific anagrams Joyce created to support the identification of his text as Alp's letter, or as "Anna's grams." The text is both the letter discovered by Biddy as she scratches in the midden heap and the midden heap itself. The link between Biddy and the gram as a scratched mark is made by the fact that "what she was *scratching* at the hour of klokking twelve looked for all this zogzag world like a goodish-sized sheet of letterpaper" (*FW* 111.7–9; emphasis added). Biddy is literally marking grams, or scratching marks, on the paper.

Of course, all writing starts from one initial scratch, or gram, and the *Wake* links this writing with reading. Both start "from scratch." When we first start reading, we "are once amore as babes awondering in a wold made fresh where with the hen in the storyaboot we start from *scratch* (*FW* 336.16–18; emphasis added). This is one of the many multiple entry points into the text for the reader, and, as one of the wandering babes in the wood/world/text, we will eventually start "feeling like [we] was lost in the bush"

(*FW* 112.3). The way in which to find our place again is to persevere in following our "poultriest notion[s]" (*FW* 112.5–6) about the wood/world of the text and let Biddy be the "kindly fowl" whose scratching will "[l]ead" (*FW* 112.9) us along one of the *Wake's* many circular, bifurcating, and interconnected paths.

In the lessons section the identification of the words of the text with a wood is strengthened by the female version of the letter "[b]y her free-written" (*FW* 280.2): "Is it in the now *woodwordings* of our sweet planta-tion where the branchings then will singingsing tomorrows gone and yesters outcome" (*FW* 280.4–7; emphasis added). The grams of the individual let-ters are divided into male and female pen strokes: "Those pothooks mostly she hawks from Poppa Vere Foster but these curly mequeues are of Mippa's moulding" (*FW* 280.16–18). Shem and Shaun as "jemmijohns" argue, or "cudgel," over arithmetic, or "a rhythmatick" (*FW* 268.7–8), but Issy has learned a female grammar for writing from her "gramma's grammar" (*FW* 268.17). The foregrounding of this female grammar is a part of the circular pattern drawing attention to the operations of the gram and identifying much of the text's language as female. It is thus a part of the *Wake's* anti-phallocentric movement and an important part of Joyce's "working over" of phallogocentrism from the side of the female.

Besides foregrounding such operations of the gram, the *Wake* also em-ploys the grams of individual letters and other symbols in a way that dis-rupts and deconstructs the traditional phonocentric functions of the letters. In *Of Grammatology*, Derrida explores some of the ways in which "[n]on-phonetic writing breaks the noun apart" and participates in the deconstruc-tion of a logocentrism that privileges "substantiality, that other metaphysi-cal name of presence and *ousia*" (Derrida 1976:26). He sees the link between the "noun and the word" in terms of the "unities of breath and concept" operating in phonocentrism. In using phonetic signifiers in a non-phonetic manner, the *Wake* moves toward the sort of "pure writing" Derr-ida sees effacing the noun and the word (Derrida 1976:26). It also produces another (and "other") doubling effect in setting phonetic signifiers to work ideogrammatically.

What Derrida uncovers in his investigation of the trace of arche-writing and what the *Wake* puts into practice with its nonphonetic uses of phonetic symbols is the "indefinitely" "becoming unmotivated" of the trace. As Derrida states it in "Saussarian language," "there is neither symbol nor sign but a becoming-sign of the symbol" (Derrida 1976:47). The traditional phonetic function of the letter "E," for example, is to symbolize the sound that is realized in the voicing of that letter. When the *Wake* places that gram on its side (*FW* 6.32) to depict "HCE interred in the landscape" (Joyce, cited in McHugh 1980:6), the letter ceases to be a phonetic symbol and becomes an ideogrammatic signifier of HCE's death and interment. This is also the case for the reversed *E* (*FW* 36.17) that loses its motivation as a phonetic symbol and becomes the ideogram for a physical gesture HCE makes by "placing [his] right fist in [his] bent left elbow" (McHugh 1980:36).

This deconstructive "becoming-unmotivated" of the phonetic symbols is described in the *Wake* as a "certain change of state of grace of nature" (*FW* 119.20) by which the "trilithon sign" (*FW* 119.17) of the *E* (placed so that its normally horizontal lines are printed vertically like an *M*) ceases to be motivated as a symbol of sound and becomes a "sign" of HCE's "title in sigla" (*FW* 119.19). The same "becoming unmotivated" can be traced in the *Wake*'s use of the Greek Δ, which becomes "fontly called . . . alp" (*FW* 119.19–20), thereby losing its function as a phonetic symbol, as well as in the operations of the other sigla used to identify the rest of the Earwicker family, the four old men, and *Finnegans Wake* itself.

The process of the siglas becoming unmotivated is at least a double process that operates according to the same doubling (and "Dublin") logic that we have already traced. Roland McHugh notes that the sigla signify not only "personages" but also "fluid composites" and "nonhuman elements" (McHugh 1976:10). The *Wake* asks "why not take the [E on its side] for a village inn"; the Δ "for an upsidown bridge"; the *x* of the four old men as "a multiplication marking for crossroads ahead"; the inverted *v* of the "pothook for the family gibbet"; the square signifying the text "for the bucker's field"; the *T* on its side "for a tryst someday"; and the square with its "onesidemissing for an allblind alley leading to an Irish plot in the Champ de Mors" (*FW* 119.27–32).

The various sigla thus lose their motivation as either symbols of sound or as symbols of the Earwicker family, the four old men and the text when they become ideogrammatic signifiers of an inn, a bridge, a multiplication mark and a crossroads, a gibbet, a field, and a tryst. They then lose this motivation when they become signifiers of the grams, or inscribed marks, of drawing or writing itself and are identified as the scribbled or "doodled" marks of the "Doodles family, ⊓, Δ, ⊣, χ , ☐, ∧, ⊏. Hoodle doodle, fam.?" (*FW* 299 F4).

Logocentrism, Phonocentrism, and Phallocentrism

While there are obviously specific links between these three terms, they are not identical and do not signify the same operations in the philosophical and literary uses of language upon which Derrida focuses in his investigations of the Western metaphysical tradition. In general terms, logocentrism signifies textual operations that are governed by traditional forms of philosophical logic (predicate logic, syllogistic logic, the logic of the dialectic, an avoidance of the various forms of fallacious reasoning, and so on) and are structured teleologically. In so far as a logocentric text attends to the operations of the *logos* as linguistic operations of the word, it can also be involved with the phonocentric operations of texts that view the primary function of written language as the representation of the spoken forms of that language.

Derrida is aware of the importance of the spoken form of the creative *logos* in the Judeo-Christian tradition (an awareness we have seen in both his theories of translation as well as in his readings of *Finnegans Wake*), but it is on the basis of Plato's writings that he elaborates many of his ideas about classical philosophical phonocentrism. In "Plato's Pharmacy," as we have seen, he explores the privileging of speech over writing that Plato establishes through his use of the Egyptian myth of the contest between Ammon Ra and Thoth. In "The Double Session," he returns to Plato's writings and examines how Socrates privileges interior thought over speech and speech over writing. Thought is superior to speech because it is internal and seems more capable of guaranteeing an interior self-presence of the thinker within the immediate presence of his or her thought. Speech is less desirable because it requires that meaning be exteriorized through phonetic articulation, but it is still more desirable than the dead letter of writing, which requires neither the presence of the speaker or listener demanded by speech nor the immediate presence of the reader in the company of the writer. In each case, the desirability of the particular linguistic form (thought, spoken or written) is determined by the philosophical concept of presence.

Phallocentrism is involved with logocentrism, and Derrida has stated that they "are indissociable," although "the stresses can lie more here or there according to the case; the force and the trajectory of the mediations can be different." Ultimately, however, a "radical dissociation between the two motifs cannot be made in all rigour." Phallogocentrism is the term with which Derrida unites phallocentrism and logocentrism. It works like one of Joyce's puns as it combines the terms for the phallus (the penis but also the model of the line), logos (thought, spoken and written words as well as classic forms of logic), and centrism. Phallogocentrism centers the operations of language around the logical and linearizing rules and models that govern them. Phallogocentrism is not, however, a monolithic edifice. Even though it is "one single thing, . . . it is an articulated thing" with innumer-

able forms of articulation that break it down into various specific articulations calling "for different strategies" (Derrida 1992b:59–60).

We saw Derrida describe double structures like those of Joyce's texts as
"violently phallocentric" yet simultaneously "produc[ing] deconstructive
effects, . . . precisely against phallocentrism, whose logic is always ready to
reverse itself" (Derrida 1992b:59). Although it is *Finnegans Wake* that most
clearly foregrounds its own deconstructive effects (including those that
work against its phallocentric story of HCE's "Phall"), the double, simultaneously phallocentric and deconstructive effects are discernible in much of
Joyce's writing.

The logic governing the Aristotelian teleology by which a unified plot
moves from its beginning through its middle to its end is disrupted by the
structures of many of the stories in *Dubliners*. The central, climactic events
that should center the stories are absent: the death of Father Flynn; the
possible masturbation in "An Encounter"; Bob Doran's seduction of Polly;
Eveline's romance with Frank; Corley's extraction of the coin from the
young woman. These and the other gaps in the stories are in part a result of
Joyce's depiction of the despair, the loneliness, and the paralysis of his characters, but this does not negate the ways in which they decenter and deconstruct the structures of these stories in such a way that the stories could
all more or less be described by the phrase from "A Painful Case":
"adventureless tale[s]" (*D* 105).

In their own ways many of the stories of *Dubliners* privilege phallocentrism in their attention to the phallus and/or the operations of the model
of the line. The world of *Dubliners* is a patriarchal world, a domestic and
social network whose economy is sustained by a capital shored up with
phallic power and precisely regulated according to the laws of the model of
the line. It is a world in which the males, who are fathers, husbands, uncles,
priests, politicians, and even the phallic maternal figures like Mrs. Mooney
and Mrs. Kearney, divide, control and rule the familial and social structures
of the stories through a phallic power. In each case such domination operates according to the model of the line as a tool of division, control, and
regulation.

Old Cotter's hints about the sexual dimension to Father Flynn's interest
in the boy; Flynn's tongue resting on his lower lip; the pervert with his
phallic walking stick and Eveline's father with his "blackthorn stick" (*D*
29); the train that carries the boy to Araby and the one that kills Emily
Sinico; the stick with which Farrington beats his son; the candle Bob Doran
lights for Polly; and even Gabriel's impulse to shield Gretta from the possible obscenities of the bottle maker: all of these are symbolic of the phallic

power that helps to shore up the capital regulating the phallocentric and linear textual economy of *Dubliners*.

At the same time as they produce this phallocentric effect, the stories deconstruct it. The pervert's possible masturbation is literally left obscene, or "off stage"; the boy's phallic quest in "Araby" ends with his painful recognition of his own vanity; Bob Doran may light Polly's candle, but we never see him light her fire; Farrington's beating of his son is rendered as an undesirable, condemnable cruelty; the actions of Mrs. Mooney and Mrs. Kearney are those of unpleasant and domineering bullies; Eveline is a victim of her father's cruel and threatening behavior; and Gabriel comes to recognize his foolishness and vanity. The phallocentric effects of the stories are thus deconstructed in such a way that they can be accurately remarked with Lily's description of the men she knows: they are all so much "palaver" (178).

Phallogocentrism is closely linked to the concept of the book as an ideological structure. The phallic model of the line that regulates and represses the "pluri-dimensional symbolic" play of thought and language is also "structurally bound up" with the possibility of "economy, of technics, and of ideology." Derrida describes a "solidarity" between these forces and the operations of the model of the line, and this solidarity manifests itself in various forms of the ideological model of the book. It "appears in the process of thesaurization, capitalization, sedentarization, hierarchization, of the formation of ideology by the class that writes or rather commands the scribes" (Derrida 1976:86).

We have already seen how Joyce's *A Portrait of the Artist as a Young Man* can be read as a kind of "grouped textual field" from which deconstruction can get under way, and the text offers numerous examples of the "enigmatic model of the line" operating as it "relaxes its oppression" of writing. The numerous shifts between the various narrative styles (a child's story; the infant Stephen's poem; the rhythm of the dance Stephen's mother plays on the piano; the third-person, past-tense narrative; the dialogues; the theological sermon; the philosophical theory of aesthetics; the confession; the first-person, present-tense diary fragments) constitute interruptions to any single linearity of style and prevent any full, phallogocentric regulation of the text by one single linear model.

At the same time, the text presents a positive deconstructive assault on the traditional ideological structure of the book in its lack of a conclusion to the story of Stephen Dedalus. To follow Stephen's story, the reader must read beyond the borders of *Portrait* and follow the development of Stephen across the textual borders of *Ulysses*. The two texts thus create a double pattern that repeats the general double of writing we have seen elsewhere at work in both Joyce and Derrida. While it is clearly possible to treat this double pattern in the traditional terms of a novel sequence in which the same characters reappear, this double structure still works toward suspending the effects of closure traditionally established with the ending and beginning of the book as an ideological structure.

In simple terms, Stephen occupies a series of double positions, and his character in *Ulysses* cannot be understood fully without a reading of *Portrait* any more than the causal effects of his actions in *Portrait* can be considered in isolation from those effects in the later work. Stephen's refusal to pray for his mother in *Ulysses,* for example, cannot be understood without some knowledge of his refusal to "make [his] easter duty" in *Portrait* (*PA* 259–60) any more than his banishment of her ghost in *Ulysses* (*U* 474–75) can be comprehended without some knowledge of his rejection of Catholicism in *Portrait*. Stephen's brandishing of his ashplant/sword to banish his mother's ghost in "Circe" is a phallocentric action, but, as the culmination of his struggle against Catholicism in *Portrait,* it is simultaneously antiphallocentric.

In other words, the teleological trajectory of Stephen's development crosses the borders of the two texts and disrupts the ideological closures of both. Furthermore, while Stephen is clearly the central figure of *Portrait* (as well as of the earlier *Stephen Hero*), his position in *Ulysses* is marginalized to such an extent that he eventually becomes little more than a figure in Molly's nocturnal meditations as Joyce's writing follows the larger trajectory in which the privileging of a male-dominated phallogocentrism becomes displaced by the *Wake*'s "languo of flows" that is ALP's maternal language.

Stephen and Bloom are both vehicles for the phallocentric impulses of Joyce's writing. Stephen's Jesuit education and Bloom's desire to make a living in the commercial world of advertising are both expressions of this phallocentrism. Stephen's education enables him to appreciate Aquinas and poetry, but it can do little more than temporarily inhibit the phallic sexual drives that manifest themselves in his voyeurism, masturbation, and copulation with prostitutes. Bloom also derives pleasure from voyeurism and masturbation, and the "Circe" episode reveals his phallic-centered, sadomasochism. Bloom may think temporarily that "[a]ll [is] gone. All fallen" (*U* 234) and temporarily "feel so lonely Bloom" (*U* 235) when he meditates on Boylan and Molly in "Sirens," but he soon recovers in order to fight with the citizen and then go on to masturbate whilst looking at Gerty and peeping at her "nainsook knickers" (*U* 300).

CHAPTER 10

A Final Frame (Up Beyond the Either) or Desire Between Joyce and Derrida

IN THE FIRST FIVE WORDS APPEARING ON page 3 of *Finnegans Wake,* Joyce's writing re-marks its own deconstructive, antiphallocentric tendencies, even though it does so within a writing that simultaneously operates according to marked phallocentric impulses. The double effects created by the simultaneously phallocentric and deconstructive forces of Joyce's earlier writing are more marked in the *Wake* because of Joyce's conscious decision to make his writing operate according to the unconscious principles and alogical patterns of the dream. *Finnegans Wake* is a much more delinearized writing than Joyce's earlier work, and this delinearization helps lift the repression of "pluri-dimensional symbolic thought" (Derrida 1976:86).

The Trigger

Restaging a release of Derrida's disseminative trigger seems as good a way as any to conclude this necessarily fragmentary reading of Derrida's reading of Joyce. No reading of Joyce, or Derrida, could ever be complete (and a reading of Joyce *and* Derrida is necessarily twice as incomplete—a sort of double incompleteness), but pulling a trigger is one way to put an end to things (as well, of course, as initiating them), if only temporarily. The metaphor of the trigger is a mechanical one, and Derrida warns: "No one is allowed on these premises if he is afraid of machines and if he still believes that literature, and perhaps even thought, ought to exorcise the machine, the two having nothing to do with each other" (Derrida 1981:292).

Exploiting *Littré*, Derrida cites several semantic values for the trigger or "*Le déclenchment.*" These include: "n. 1. The automatic release of a mechanism. 2. Any device in a position to engage or to stop the moving parts of a machine. 3. The act of triggering the motion of a machine by means of such a device" (Derrida 1981:290). Whether as a "clappercoupling smelting-works" (*FW* 614.30–31), an "autokinaton" (*FW* 235.27), a "*bairdboard bombardment screen*" (*FW* 349.8), or an "airish chaunting car" (*FW* 55.24), *Finnegans Wake* offers numerous metaphors with which it identifies itself as some kind of machine. The various accounts of the event in the park also bring into play the specific killing machine of the revolver that HCE has "placed to his face" (*FW* 62.32).

At the level of the text's narrative concerning the events that take place in the park, it is unclear if HCE is shot or merely threatened with the revolver, or if the shot from the revolver is HCE's sexual ejaculation. Issy's comments in the lessons section suggest the latter. "Am shot, says the big-guard" (*FW* 260.6–7), and Issy's remarks on this exclamation reveal her knowledge that being shot by HCE in this way would result in her pregnancy: "If old *H*erod with the Corm-well's *e*czema was to go for me like he does Snuffler whatever about his blue canaries *I'd do nine months* for his beaver beard" (*FW* 260 F1; emphasis added).

At the level of the *Wake*'s foregrounding of its own writing and the operations of its grammar, the trigger is both that of a simultaneously phallic and mechanical revolver *and* the kind of textual mechanism that Derrida sees putting textual operations in motion. This trigger fires off another double operation. It sets writing to work at the level of the narrative *and* in the simultaneous deconstructive re-marking of its own textuality: "The story that seems to be thus triggered off . . . then begins to function according to modalities in which death is affiliated with the (metaphor of the) textual machine" (Derrida 1981:292). In the *Wake,* the trigger of the revolver that threatens HCE and symbolizes his phallus is also the trigger that allows writing to operate.

Following the question "How used you learn me, brather . . . ?" (*FW* 468.3–4), the *Wake* offers a catalog of grammatical and poetic terms, including a deconstructed passage grafted from Kennedy's *Latin Primer* (McHugh 1980:468) that constitutes a "trigger" setting the grammatical operations of the text in motion: "Thou the first person shingeller. Art, an imperfect subjunctive. . . . Miss Smith onamatterpoetic. Hammis-andivis axes colles waxes warmas like sodullas [the graft from the *Primer*]. So pick your stops with fondnes snow. And mind you twine the twos noods of your nicenames. And pull up your furbelovs as far-above as you're farthingales. That'll hint him how to click the *trigger*" (*FW* 468. 8–15; emphasis added). This trigger is also the trigger of a revolver pulled by a "finger" (Gk. *daktylizô*): "So dactylise him up to blankpoint" (*FW* 468.16–17). To "dactylise" repeats the process of putting writing to work according to the rhythm of a metrical pattern *and* that of using a finger to pull the trigger of a gun at "blankpoint," or "point-blank," range. Derrida re-marks this kind of double operation by which writing is simultaneously involved with repetition and death: "Born of repetition . . . even in its first occurrence, the text mechanically, mortally reproduces . . . the process of its own triggering" (Derrida 1981:292).

First trigger release: "riverrun, past Eve and Adam's" (*FW* 3.1): Roland McHugh identifies both the pun on *erinnerung* (G. "remembrance") and the name of Dublin's Adam and Eve's Church as well as the tavern of the same name. When the reader reaches ALP's plaintive cry "mememormee" (*FW* 628.14), he can recognize the repetition of this cry for remembrance in the "riverrun"/*erinnerung* pun. "[R]iverrun" functions as a deconstructive trigger: it sets the text in motion by proclaiming the simultaneous flow of the river Liffey and the *Wake's* "languo of flows" while completing the cyclical pattern of the *Wake* by repeating ALP's closing plea to be remembered. It also puns on the Anglo-Irish pronunciation of "reverend," triggering the mechanism of the letter, or "epistolear," (*FW* 38.23) which ALP as "[o]ur cad's bit of strife" (*FW* 38.9) whispers as "gossiple" (*FW* 38.23) into the ear of "her particular *reverend,* the director" (*FW* 38.18–19; emphasis added). This version of the letter repeats the events that transpire in the park, including the involvement of the revolver or pistol, and "epistolear" triggers the repetition of the letter, (epistle), the revolver (pistol), and ALP's words to HCE as she speaks them to his ear ("epistol*ear*"; emphasis added).

Second trigger release: "past Eve and Adam's" interrupts the linearity of

"Adam and Eve's." It does so by reversing the positions of Adam and Eve and putting Eve in an initial and, according to the logic of linearity, primary position. The first male human is thus displaced, and the first female human takes his place. This antiphallocentric movement repeats the one we have seen in which "the Lord God, who is and was and who is to come" (Rev. 1.8) is replaced by the words of "Anna was, Livia is, Plurabelle's to be" (*FW* 215.24) and "Mammy was, Mimmy is, Minuscoline's to be" (*FW* 226.14–15). Because its language is signed as a female language, the *Wake* declares, "The word is my Wife" (*FW* 167.29).

With "past Eve and Adam's," Joyce's writing completes a trajectory that began with *Stephen* Dedalus as a *Hero,* then moved through the male positions of Dedalus and Bloom (with the frequently phallocentric effects of those positions) in order to arrive at the double female position that simultaneously closes *Ulysses* and brings writing into the night language that is the "nat" language of the *Wake.* "Past Eve and Adam's" bids farewell to the male position as the dominant position in language. The "riverrun" is not about Stephen and tells us so in the pun "*pas* (Fr. 'not') Stephen" ("past Eve and"/"*pas*" Stephen). A third pun may also identify ALP, or Anna, with the historical, or "past," Eve ("past Eve and Adam's"/"past Eve Ann"). According to the *Wake*'s puns and double (Dublin and "doublin") logic, even the male name, Adam, can be read as a re-marking of this farewell to the dominant masculine position. Using the antiphallocentric technique of "caps ever[ing]" taught in the lessons section, the proper name "Adam" can also be read and heard as "a dam," re-marking the maternal status of ALP and her "riverrun."

Third trigger release: "riverrun" sets in motion the text's network of liquid metaphors. The most extensive analysis of the various liquids in the *Wake* is provided by Margaret Solomon's *Eternal Geomater: The Sexual Universe of* Finnegans Wake (Solomon 1969). Solomon does not foreground a use of deconstruction, but her reading maps out many of the simultaneously phallocentric and antiphallocentric movements in Joyce's text. Tracing the associative chains of liquids in the text (water, river, rain, whiskey, beer, porter, tea, ink, urine, semen, and so on), her study allows us to recognize that HCE *is* Adam and Eve's tavern (the "village inn" [*FW* 119.27]; the "Mullingcan Inn" [*FW* 64.9]; the lessons section's double "Inn inn!" [*FW* 262.26]), where porter is dispensed as well the character who micturates in the park. His urine is associated with the ink, semen, and tea found in Shem's "teatimestained terminal" (*FW* 114.29–30), and tea (which puns on the phallic *T*) is "not only feminine urine [like the prankquean's] but also male semen" (Solomon 1969:78).

This (con)fusion of liquids sustains the metaphor of the liquidity of the *Wake*'s language, making it ultimately impossible to distinguish, with any precision, between the phallocentric and antiphallocentric impulses of Joyce's writing. HCE's fall as a phallic "Phall" (*FW* 4.15), for example, simultaneously marks both HCE's use of the creative and sexual powers that lead to his fall and the failure that the use of them produces. When the prankquean rains (and reigns) over "Woeman's Land" (*FW* 22.8), she occupies the phallogocentric position of one who rules, but the third time that she urinates at Jarl von Hoother's door and inflames his desire (she again "pull[s] a rosy one. . . . and fire-land was ablaze" [*FW* 21.15–17]), Jarl becomes erect "to the whole length of the strength of his bowman's bill" (*FW* 23.2–3). He enters the door, or "port," of the prankquean, and as he "ports" "her," or penetrates her, they create "the first peace of illiterative *porthery* in all the flamend floody flatuous world" (*FW* 23.9–10; emphasis added).

Fourth trigger release: "As soon as writing, which entails making a liquid flow out of a tube on to a piece of white paper assumes the significance of copulation . . . writing . . . [is] stopped because [it] represent[s] the performance of a forbidden sexual act" (Freud cited in Derrida 1976:xlvii–iii). Derrida's work reveals a strong awareness of Freud's understanding of the thinking, speaking, and writing of literature and philosophy as processes made possible by the sublimation of the drives, and much of his interest in Joyce re-marks the ways in which Joyce maps out the relationships between the operations of desire and its objects as the double structure of a writing that re-marks the operations of its own "other" within itself. In simple terms, it is the distance between the desiring subject and its desired object(s) that allows desire to operate.

One of the tropes for the double of writing traced by the *Wake*'s prankquean episode is that in which desire is simultaneously involved its own failure. It is simultaneously a desiring and a de-desiring (or de-sire-ing) process. When the prankquean arrives at the castle, Jarl is on two occasions masturbating (first "laying cold hands on himself" [*FW* 21.11] and then "shaking warm hands with himself" [*FW* 21.36]). His desire is obviously for sexual gratification, but it is not a desire to sire a child with the "other" of the prankquean. Her desire repels Jarl so much that he twice shuts the door in her face.

Only on the prankquean's third visit does Jarl decide to come into her "like the campbells acoming with a fork lance of lightning" (*FW* 22.30–31). At this point, the forces of human desire are set in motion in a simultaneous act of specific copulation between Jarl and the prankquean and a sublimation of universal human desire in the synthesis of the four Classical, primal elements of fire, water, earth, and wind with the religious myths of the ritualistic flooding and apocalyptic burning of the world: "that was the first peace of illiterative porthery in all the flamend floody flatuous world" (*FW* 23.9–10). Epic in its scope (it catalogs the "flame," "water," "wind," and "earth" of Classical thought and synthesizes these with the biblical "flood" and the apocalyptic "flamend" of the earth), this synthesis is also anti-epic in its condensation of these events within a single sentence. What this single sentence undermines is the linearity and historicity of the numerous, temporally structured, historical narratives of Classical thought and Judeo-Christian myths that Joyce fuses together throughout his "collideorscape."

(In)conclusions

The preface to this study cites Stephen Heath's argument that "[t]here is no conclusion to be reached in a reading of Joyce's text" (Heath 1984:61). One viable way of temporarily finishing or suspending a reading of Joyce's text is to learn Joyce's own technique of reading as "raiding" (*FW* 482.32), and this Heath does in raiding the *Wake* and *Epiphanies* for appropriate passages with which to close his own reading: "The end? Say it with missiles then and thus arabesque the page" (*FW* 115.2–3; Heath 1984:61).

Even this is unsatisfactory, however, as Heath points out: "an ambi-violent extension of [Joyce's] text in a new practice of writing is beyond the scope of the present simple introduction" (Heath 1984:61). Heath ends his study with a passage from *Epiphanies* in which he sees Joyce "resuming . . . in the account of a dream, in relation to origin and language and subject, the clouding of the 'Cartesian spring'." The passage Heath cites provides an analogy for reading a beast of a text that is written in a language that cannot be understood: "Something is moving in the pool; it is an arctic beast with a rough yellow coat. I thrust in my stick and as he rises out of the water I see that his back slopes towards the croup and that he is very sluggish. I am not afraid but, thrusting at him often with my stick drive him before me. He moves his paws heavily and mutters words of some language which I do not understand" (Heath 1984:61–62).

In the same year that Heath attempted to deal with the problem of closure in a reading of Joyce, Patrick Parrinder considered the problem from a more historical perspective. His view is that some of Joyce's linguistic experiments in the *Wake* "may, at some points, have gone astray" (Parrinder 1984:237). Parrinder shares the rather pessimistic view expressed earlier by

Bernard Benstock in *Joyce-Again's Wake:* "Time, which was expected to bring all evidence eventually to the surface in an ordered pattern, so far has had the opposite effect" (Benstock 1965:40). Parrinder sees the difficulties of understanding the *Wake* increasing as the period of Joyce's life becomes more historically distant: "As Joyce's lifetime recedes from us, and with it the likelihood of recovering those of his more fugitive and ephemeral allusions which have yet to be detected, the *Wake* is in some ways getting more difficult, even as scholarship renders it easier to master" (Parrinder 1984:236).

Both Benstock and Parrinder view Joyce's achievements from the perspectives afforded by their positions as eminent scholars. These perspectives are necessarily grounded in, and governed by, the historical and teleological models of research and development that determine and regulate academic, scholarly research. Derrida's readings of Joyce offer an alternative to such a perspective. Where many traditional scholars see the discovery and cataloging of Joyce's allusions and references as one of the most essential (if not *the* most essential task) of studying Joyce, even traditional scholars like Parrinder recognize that many traditional forms of scholarship (breaking down Joyce's puns into their component "*etym*[s]," tracking down his allusions, establishing the concordances, lexicons, catalogs, and other taxonomies for his writing) may not be the only ways (or even the most desirable ways) of reading Joyce. This is because the "encyclopaedic nature of [the] knowledge" with which Joyce made the *Wake* a "history of the world" is arranged in ways that show Joyce "had utterly abandoned any preconceived ideas of a canon or hierarchy of knowledge" (Parrinder 1984:237).

The philosophy upon which much literary scholarship is grounded is the traditional, logical, and teleological philosophy that Derrida terms phallogocentrism. It is a philosophy that rarely considers the model of the line with which it produces its own logical and rhetorical categories and creates its taxonomic systems. Discussing the operations of this model of the line within the context of the history of philosophy, Derrida argues that the "enigmatic model of the *line* is . . . the very thing that philosophy could not see when it had its eyes open on the interiority of its own history" (Derrida 1976:86). This model of the line also would enable those whom Parrinder terms "orthodox historians" to draw a line between acceptable elements in Joyce's "history of the world" and those they "would see as trivial and ephemeral" (Parrinder 1984:237).

There are few critics who would deny that Joyce is in some ways an epic writer, but Derrida's reading of Joyce reveals another order at work in

Joyce's writings. This is the "order" that, the *Wake* tells us, "[o]nly is . . . othered" in Joyce's text (*FW* 613.13–14). The Aristotelian model of temporal linearity by which past, present, and future are conceived in terms of a past-present, a present-present, and a future-present is "othered" in the simulacrum of a temporal sequence with which the *Wake* interrogates the presentation of character in language: "Yet is no body present here which was not there before" (613.13). The double present of Joyce's writing that enables a body to be present "here" at the same time that it was "there before" simultaneously assaults the concept of representation and the linear and temporal model that can be explored within the context of those "revolutions" in "philosophy, in science [and] in literature" that "can be interpreted as shocks that are gradually destroying the linear model. Which is to say the *epic* model" (Derrida 1976:87).

Within the context of Derrida's deconstructive project (which is in many places a re-marking of Joyce's achievements and his haunting of Derrida's), the access to the symbolic aspects of pluri-dimensional writing made possible by Joyce is much more than a "simple regression toward the 'mythogram'" (Derrida 1976:87). Joyce's writing frequently uses "mythograms," but these are often overdetermined so that Stephen Dedalus can be Hamlet and Telemachus, and Bloom can be both Odysseus and Old Hamlet. HCE can be fallen humanity, Humpty Dumpty, and Humphrey Chimpden Earwicker, and ALP can be a mother, a lover, a wife, a bridge, an alp, and the history of Western language. *Finnegans Wake* is simultaneously an epic and an anti-epic. During the eleven or so years that it took to write *Ulysses* and the seventeen years it took to write *Finnegans Wake,* Joyce learned to imitate innumerable writers and styles. These he forged into a unique style that has no equal in this century. The "epical forged cheque" that Joyce as "Vulgariano . . . utter[ed] . . . on the public for his own private profit" (*FW* 181.14–16) "makes all the rationality subjected to the linear model appear as another form and another age of mythography." Derrida marks out this appearing as he reads it writing itself in its own disappearance "between the lines" of Joyce (Derrida 1976:87, 86).

BIBLIOGRAPHY

Attridge, Derek. 1992a. "This Strange Institution Called Literature: An Interview with Jacques Derrida." In *Acts of Literature,* edited by Derek Attridge, 33–75. New York: Routledge.

———. 1992b. Editor's introduction. "*Ulysses* Gramophone: Hear Say Yes in Joyce." In *Acts of Literature,* edited by Derek Attridge, 253–56. New York: Routledge.

Bass, Alan. 1978. "Introduction." In *Writing and Difference,* by Jacques Derrida, ix–xx. Trans. Alan Bass. Chicago: University of Chicago Press.

Bennington, Geoffrey. 1984. "Translator's Notes." "Two Words for Joyce." In *Poststructuralist Joyce: Essays from the French,* edited by Derek Attridge and Daniel Ferrer, 158–59. Cambridge: Cambridge University Press.

———. 1994. *Legislations: The Politics of Deconstruction.* London and New York: Verso.

Bennington, Geoffrey, and Jacques Derrida. 1993. *Jacques Derrida.* Trans. G. Bennington. Chicago: University of Chicago Press.

Benstock, Bernard. 1965. *Joyce-Again's Wake.* Seattle and London: University of Washington Press.

Benstock, Shari. 1983. "At the Margin of Discourse: Footnotes in the Fictional Text." *PMLA* 98 (2): 204–24.

———. 1984. "The Letter of the Law: *La Carte Postale in Finnegans Wake.*" *Philological Quarterly* 63 (spring): 163–85.

Blake, William. 1982. *The Complete Poetry and Prose of William Blake.* Ed. David V. Erdman. New York: Anchor Books.

Bloom, Harold. 1973. *The Anxiety of Influence: A Theory of Poetics.* New York: Oxford University Press.

———. 1994. *The Western Canon: The Books and School of the Ages.* London: Papermac.

Connolly, Thomas E., ed. 1961. *James Joyce's Scribbledehobble: The Ur-Workbook for* Finnegans Wake. Evanston, Ill.: Northwestern University Press.

Derrida, Jacques. 1976. *Of Grammatology.* Trans. Gayatri Chakravorty Spivak. Baltimore: Johns Hopkins University Press.

———. 1978. *Writing and Difference.* Trans. Alan Bass. Chicago: University of Chicago Press.

———. 1979. "Scribble (writing-power)." Trans. Cary Plotkin. *Yale French Studies* 58: 116–47.

———. 1981. *Dissemination.* Trans. Barbara Johnson. Chicago: University of Chicago Press.

———. 1982. "Différance." In *Margins of Philosophy,* trans. Alan Bass, 1–27. Chicago: University of Chicago Press.

———. 1984a. "Two Words for Joyce." Trans. G. Bennington. *Post-structuralist Joyce: Essays from the French,* edited by Derek Attridge and Daniel Ferrer. Cambridge: Cambridge University Press.

———. 1984b. "Of an Apocalyptic Tone Recently Adopted in Philosophy." *T.O.L.R.* 6 (2): 3–37.

———. 1986a. *Glas.* Trans. John P. Leavey Jr. and Richard Rand. Lincoln: University of Nebraska Press.

———. 1986b. "Proverb: 'He that would pun . . . '." *Glassary,* by John P. Leavey Jr., 17–20. Lincoln: University of Nebraska Press.

———. 1987a. *The Post Card: From Socrates to Freud and Beyond.* Trans. Alan Bass. Chicago: University of Chicago Press.

———. 1987b. *Positions.* Trans. Alan Bass. London: Athlone Press.

———. 1987c. *Ulysse gramophone: Deux mots pour Joyce.* Paris: Galilée.

———. 1989. *Edmund Husserl's* Origin of Geometry: *An Introduction.* Trans. J. P. Leavy Jr. Lincoln: University of Nebraska Press.

———. 1992a. "*Ulysses* Gramophone: Hear Say Yes in Joyce." In *Acts of Literature,* edited by Derek Attridge, 253–309. New York: Routledge.

———. 1992b. "'This Strange Institution Called Literature': An Interview with Jacques Derrida." With Derek Attridge. In *Acts of Literature,* edited by Derek Attridge, 33–75. New York: Routledge.

———. 1994. *Specters of Marx: The State of the Debt, the Work of Mourning, and the New International.* Trans. Peggy Kamuf. Ed. Bernd Magnus and Stephen Cullenberg. New York: Routledge.

Eco, Umbero. 1979. "The Semantics of Metaphor." In *The Role of the Reader: Explorations in the Semiotics of Texts,* 67–89. Bloomington: Indiana University Press.

Ellmann, Richard. 1983. *James Joyce.* Oxford: Oxford University Press.

Eysteinsson, Astradur. 1990. *The Concept of Modernism.* Ithaca: Cornell University Press.

Gasché, Rodolphe. 1986. *The Tain of the Mirror: Derrida and the Philosophy of Reflection.* Cambridge: Harvard University Press.

Gilbert, Stuart. 1963. *James Joyce's* Ulysses. Harmondsworth: Penguin.

Handelman, Susan. 1982. *The Slayers of Moses: The Emergence of Rabbinic Interpretation in Modern Literary Theory*. New York: New York State University Press.

Hart, Clive. 1963. *A Concordance to* Finnegans Wake. Minneapolis: University of Minnesota Press.

Hartman, Geoffrey. 1981. *Saving the Text: Literature/ Derrida/ Philosophy*. Baltimore: Johns Hopkins University Press.

Heath, Stephen. 1984. "Ambiviolences: Notes for Reading Joyce." In *Post-structuralist Joyce: Essays from the French*, edited by Derek Attridge and Daniel Ferrer, 31–68. Cambridge: Cambridge University Press.

Hegel, G. W. F. 1977. *Phenomenology of Spirit*. Trans. A. V. Miller. Oxford: Oxford University Press.

Johnson, Barbara. 1981. "Introduction" and "Notes." In *Dissemination,* by Jacques Derrida. Trans. B Johnson. Chicago: University of Chicago Press.

Jones, Ellen Carol. 1988. "Introduction." "Deconstructive Criticism of Joyce." In *James Joyce: The Augmented Ninth*, edited by Bernard Benstock. Syracuse: Syracuse University Press.

Joyce, James. 1982. *Finnegans Wake*. New York: Viking Press and Penguin.

———. 1983. *Giacomo Joyce*. London: Faber and Faber.

———. 1986. *Ulysses*. Ed. Hans Walter Gabler. Harmondsworth: Penguin.

———. 1992a. *A Portrait of the Artist as a Young Man*. London: Penguin.

———. 1992b. *Dubliners*. London: Penguin.

Lacan, Jacques. 1978. *The Four Fundamental Concepts of Psycho-Analysis*. Trans. Alan Sheridan. New York: W. W. Norton.

Leavey, J. P., Jr. 1986. *Glossary*. Lincoln: University of Nebraska Press.

———. 1989. "Preface" and "Coda." In *Edmund Husserl's* Origin of Geometry: *An Introduction,* by Jacques Derrida, 1–21, 181–92. Trans. J. P. Leavey Jr. Lincoln: University of Nebraska Press.

Lernout, Geert. 1990. *The French Joyce*. Ann Arbor: University of Michigan Press.

Loesberg, Jonathan. 1991. *Aestheticism and Deconstruction: Pater, Derrida, and De Man*. Princeton: Princeton University Press.

McArthur, Murray. 1995. "The Example of Joyce: Derrida Reading Joyce." *JJQ* 32 (winter): 227–41.

McHugh, Roland. 1976. *The Sigla of* Finnegans Wake. London: Edward Arnold.

———. 1980. *Annotations to* Finnegans Wake. Baltimore: Johns Hopkins University Press.

Norris, Christopher. 1987. *Derrida*. London: Fontana.

Norris, Margot. 1974. *The Decentered Universe of* Finnegans Wake: *A Structuralist Analysis*. Baltimore: Johns Hopkins University Press.

Parrinder, Patrick. 1984. *James Joyce*. Cambridge: Cambridge University Press.

Plato. 1961. "Philebus." Trans. R. Hackforth. In *The Collected Dialogues of Plato*, edited by Edith Hamilton and Huntington Cairns, 1086–1150. Bollingen Series 71. Princeton: Princeton University Press.

Solomon, Margaret C. 1969. *Eternal Geomater: The Sexual Universe of* Finnegans Wake. Carbondale: Southern Illinois University Press.

Spivak, Gayatri Chakravorty. 1976. "Translator's Preface." In *Of Grammatology,* by Jacques Derrida, ix–xc. Trans. G. C. Spivak. Baltimore: Johns Hopkins University Press.

Storey, John. 1993. *An Introductory Guide to Cultural Theory and Popular Culture.* Hemel Hempstead: Harvester Wheatsheaf.

Tindall, William York. 1969. *A Reader's Guide to* Finnegans Wake. London: Thames and Hudson.

van Boheemen, Christine. 1988. "Deconstruction after Joyce." In *New Alliances in Joyce Studies: "When It's Aped to Foul a Delfian,"* edited by Bonnie Kime Scott, 29–36. Newark: University of Delaware Press.

INDEX

Aristotle: plot structure of, xvii, 26, 101, 116; temporal model of, 126
Arnold, Matthew, 16, 17, 19
Artaud, Antonin, 81
Attridge, Derek, 41, 60, 61, 70, 76
Aubert, Jacques, 11
Augustine, Saint, 18

Babel, 37, 38, 40, 53, 62, 63–66, 85, 109
Bataille, Georges, 26–27, 81
being, xiii–xiv, 9–10, 12, 13, 94, 105
Bennington, Geoffrey, 1, 18, 44, 46, 60
Benstock, Bernard, 125
Benstock, Shari, xviii–xix, 33, 38, 40; "At the Margins of Discourse," 55; "The Letter of the Law: *La Carte Postale* in *Finnegans Wake*," 34–38
binary opposition, xviii, 59, 91, 92, 103, 104
Blake, William, xx, 93
Bloom, Harold, 92, 106
book, as ideological structure, xvi, 20–27, 32, 42, 57, 101–2, 117–18
Bruno, Giordano, 66

cogito: Cartesian, 12–16, 33–34
Cohn, Robert Greer, 65
cultural studies, xi
cultural theory, xiv–xv
culture, 4, 6, 22, 49, 56, 79, 91

David, Alain, 11
de Man, Paul, 43
Descartes, René, 12–13. *See also* cogito: Cartesian
Derrida, Jacques: arche-writing in, 91, 95–96, 103; blank in, 91, 92, 96–100; contamination in, 25, 28, 52; deconstruction in, xi–xvi, 21, 54–55, 58, 59, 62, 65, 76–79, 81, 83, 90–94, 101–2, 104–5, 116, 119; différance in, 91, 95, 103–5; double bind in, 38, 49, 62, 90; double marks in, xiii, xvi, 25, 62, 90, 91, 92, 106–10; erasure in, xiii, 10, 95; fold, 98; graft, 110–11; gram, 91, 92, 111–14; logocentrism in, 104, 112, 114–16; phallocentrism in, 14, 82, 83–88, 112, 113, 114–18, 119, 122; phallogo-centrism in, 55, 84, 85, 87, 88, 104, 112, 115–18, 125; phonocentrism in, 114–15; trace in, 91, 96, 103; trigger in, 92, 120–23; undecidables of, 19, 22, 90–118
—*Works:* "Circumfessions," 53; "Cogito and the History of Madness," 12–16; *Dissemination,* xviii, 20–31, 33, 37, 65, 108, 110; "Double Session, The," 21, 54, 64, 96, 115; *Edmund Husserl's 'Origin of Geometry': An Introduction,* 1–8; "Force and Signification," 10–12; *Glas,* xviii, 18, 20, 26, 44–57; "Implications,"